LIBRARIES FOR TODAY
AND TOMORROW

LIBRARIES FOR TODAY AND TOMORROW

HOW DO WE PAY FOR THEM?

WHO USES THEM?

WHO STAFFS THEM?

WHAT ARE THEIR SERVICES?

by Virginia H. Mathews

with an introduction by Allie Beth Martin,
President of the American Library Association

1976
Doubleday & Company, Inc., Garden City, New York

Library of Congress Cataloging in Publication Data

Mathews, Virginia H.
  Libraries for today and tomorrow.

  Includes index.
  1. Libraries—United States—History. 2. Library finance—
United States. I. Title.
Z731.M336   021'.00973

Library of Congress Catalog Card Number 75-25440
ISBN 0-385-05564-1
Copyright © 1976 by Virginia H. Mathews
All Rights Reserved
Printed in the United States of America
First Edition

For Aunty
Phyllis Inslee Hopper
For me, the best
librarian of all

Doubleday has always had a keen interest in the dedication and the responsibilities of the thousands of librarians serving in schools and public libraries. We hope that the information in this book will be of some assistance and will supply information not readily available from other sources.

NELSON DOUBLEDAY

CONTENTS

INTRODUCTION

What are the expectations for libraries for the future? Some say the expectations have never been more promising. Others cry doom and prophesy only the gloomiest future. Which will be correct? Probably neither. Or perhaps both may be right depending on the differing expectations of those eyeballing the future. This book provides concise background so necessary to assess our expectations realistically.

It begins by sketching the historic background against which libraries in America have developed. This perspective is sometimes missing in analyses of how libraries have come to be as they are today. Herein we are provided the outline of history from which emerges the manifest need for knowledge which is basic in American society. The history of American libraries which follows describes the response to this need for knowledge. Recent history, the decades of the nineteen fifties and sixties, found the acceleration of library development at its apex. Mathews summarizes the period of rapid development and the impact of federal funds.

And what has been the outcome? How are libraries serving people today as an outgrowth of their history? The description of exemplary services identified in all types of libraries indicates that expectations for the future may indeed be unlimited if the samples of the best of contemporary service become the norm rather than the exception. Recent library history, fraught with struggle and disappointment, brings the book to its final and crucial chapter and a realistic analysis of the need for planning such as is now provided by the National Commission on Libraries and Information Science. Unlike most studies of libraries past and future, which often close with unanswered questions or limited solutions, Mathews proposes specific recommendations which build on recent studies and plans of library associations and of the National Commission. She goes beyond these and stresses grass-roots networking and a new standard for library financial support: ten dollars per capita for all public libraries and ten dollars per student for all school and college libraries *plus* additional support to networks. Grass-root networks are still fragile in most of the country, many libraries country-wide do not meet the ten-dollar support standard but if these recommendations were implemented our expectations would indeed be on the way to being unlimited.

Allie Beth Martin
Tulsa, Oklahoma

Chapter I: Some Social Context for the Need to Know

Since Colonial times Americans have shown a need to know, a hunger for information about what was going on beyond what they could see and hear for themselves. For the most part uprooted to come here in the first place, we have ever been restless and mobile, ready to move on, to try something new. This way of life built individual and national self-esteem, whetted the appetite for choices and options, lent the courage and self-confidence to resist pressures, and to turn the tide against the seemingly inevitable. It also helped to develop the hunger for knowledge.

Since the twentieth century began, however, we have been all but overwhelmed by living in an almost continuous state of suspense and crisis. The up and down swoops of the social roller coaster have become more pronounced since the century entered and proceeded through its second half. The danger now appears to be that events are "coming at" people so fast that many have lost, or are losing, their desire to inquire, to assess, to decide or to assent before being swept along, powerless, by forces they might control if they knew how.

Without question, there were upheavals, violence, and deep uncertainties in American life during the eighteenth, nineteenth, and early twentieth centuries. But there seem, at least in retrospect, to have been longer periods of calm, of "normalcy," between them. And perhaps this appearance of normalcy in the past is at the heart of much that troubles people now, for we have lost the illusion that "normal" times will come again. We have even lost our definition of what "normal" is. "Normal" has been dissolved by awareness of the problems that used to be swept under the rug during the calm between ugly eruptions.

Right up until several years after the end of World War II, the disruptions of wars, massacres, riots, panics, scandals, and other assorted ills were thought of as abnormalities—interruptions of the even flow of pleasant living for those "solid citizens" who counted. America sang, "When This Cruel War Is Over," while the Civil War raged. We "waited out" the Great Depression, knowing grimly that we must hang on until it ended. We foreclosed on personal dreams "for the duration" while World War II swept over the world, knowing that they would all come true "after the War."

It was only at about the midpoint of the century—1950 —that we faced the fact that the days we had been waiting for, the feeling of security we longed for, might never come at all. There would be no closure, perhaps no satisfaction even, in the future. We have behind us now a quarter century of disillusionment, and its effects are showing.

Certainly, our century has had no monopoly on violence and insensitivity to human suffering; on violations of individual freedom; on crooked officials and chicanery in high places; on citizen rebellion, or citizen indifference. There has been plenty of it recorded. Newspapers, always a vital and until recently almost the only source of news for event-oriented Americans, have been expanding and popularizing their coverage since the 1830s. The difference, in the last half of our century is one of scale, as well as of inescapability. The news, good and bad, has manifested as a part of daily life for all the people, since the 1950s, and its effects are all-pervasive, its immediacy intrusive.

For instance, several hundred men in three Pennsylvania counties—Northampton, Bucks, and Montgomery—staged an uprising in 1799 against the Federal Property Taxes established by law in July of the previous year. Their leader, one John Gries, was convicted and sentenced to death, but was pardoned by the President, John Adams. It was probably not the subject of much family discussion at dinner, since most people probably did not hear of it until some days—or even weeks—later.

Young America was badly shaken but took it in stride, when its Vice-President, Aaron Burr (who had tied with Jefferson in popular votes in the election of 1800, and became our third Vice-President after the House of Representatives broke the tie and chose Jefferson as President), murdered his fellow statesman and political leader, Alexander Hamilton, in a duel, and later undertook some alleged treasonous activity.

Momentous events produced both good and evil outcomes. Foremost among these was the purchase from France in 1803, by President Jefferson, of the 828,000 square miles that lay between the Mississippi River and the Rockies. An exploring party, headed by Meriwether Lewis and William Clark, was sent by the President and Congress to map the territory. It is doubtful that many families, albeit interested, felt much affected, and the implications of this huge addition to America must have seemed remote to the average working man, if they did not escape him entirely.

Yet the Louisiana Purchase set the stage for the wealth and power of a great nation. Grimly, it also precipitated ferocious racial warfare against the Indians, who happened to have prior rights to life on the great plains and prairies.

There was a visible, disturbing result of the westward avalanche of European whites: an economic panic caused by wild speculation in land, overextended credit. In 1820, James Monroe was elected for a second term as President. But intrigues plagued the Cabinet, as Secretary of War John C. Calhoun and Secretary of the Treasury William H. Crawford consumed themselves and the constructive efforts of the Administration with their presidential ambitions.

In 1828, the Workingmen's Party was organized in Philadelphia, and its members agitated for free public education as well as protection against competition from prison contract labor. The ten-hour working day, initiated in

1836, did not become a national standard until the late 1850s, while workers in the New England mills continued to work eleven- and twelve-hour days until even later.

Another financial crisis in 1837 saw demonstrations by the unemployed, "protesting against the high rents and the inflated prices of food stuffs and fuel," and we are told that "a mob broke in to the city's flour warehouse and sacked the supplies." This happened in New York, where the banks also suspended business, followed by banks in Baltimore, Philadelphia, and Boston.

Abolitionist controversy in Congress began early in the nineteenth century, fired anew each time a state applied for admission to the Union. The Mexican War, 1846-48—one of the shabbier chapters in our history— groomed a generation of officers to fight. They were to find ample opportunity on both sides in the Civil War and meantime practiced their military arts with patriotic fervor against the Indians.

The Civil War period was one particularly productive of violence in America. A mob attacked the Massachusetts militia as it passed through Baltimore en route to join the Union forces in Washington, D.C.; four soldiers were killed, thirty-six wounded. It took some time for Maryland to decide whether to come into the conflict on the Union side, or remain "neutral" and thereby effectively sympathetic to the Confederacy. Nor were the provisions of the Bill of Rights always observed, even for white citizens: during the struggle for the state of Maryland, the federal government felt obliged to suspend the right of habeas corpus, and arrested and punished state and local officials who stood firm in their commitment to the South.

Between 1860 and 1865, prices rose well over 100 per cent, wages less than 50 per cent. A flow of immigrants kept the northern war machine humming, and the war spurred the adoption of labor-saving devices by industry. The Homestead Act, passed in 1862 and basically a wartime strategic measure, was to have far-reaching results. The idea was to promote speedy agricultural expansion, and provide bumper crops, of wheat especially, not only for home demand but to increase the North's bargaining power with European countries and prevent them from helping the Confederacy. The Act offered any citizen who was head of a family and over twenty-one 160 acres of surveyed land for a small registration fee and six months to five years of continuous working of the land.

A related strategy, inspired by wartime needs, was of central importance to the foundation of an educational system, and thereby to the subject of this book. This was passage, also in 1862 of the Morrill Act, by which each *loyal* state was granted land for the purpose of endowing at least one agricultural college—thus "land-grant" colleges. Under the provisions of this act, at least sixty-nine such colleges were established, major building blocks toward the American dream for the children of farm communities in the Middle and Far West. Later elaborations and extensions of federal government responsibility for higher and continuing adult education (The Hatch Act of 1887 which provided subsidies for creation of state agricultural experiment stations; the Smith-Lever Act of 1914 by which federal grants-in-aid were to be matched by state appropriations for a program of agricultural extension work carried out by the land-grant colleges in collaboration with the Department of Agriculture; and the Smith-Hughes Act of 1917 which established a Federal Board for Vocational Education, and promoted instruction in agriculture and the trades), set the precedent, not only for federal aid to education in the formal sense, but to informal, individual, independent learning for adults.

The draft riots in New York in 1863 saw four days of pillaging and rioting, and the lynching of a great many Blacks, by those who blamed them for the war, and who saw the conscription laws as favoring the rich, and unfair to the poor. According to those laws, all men from twenty years of age through forty-five were ordered up *except* those who could pay three hundred dollars, or get a substitute to serve for three years in their stead.

News of President Lincoln's assassination was probably as fast-spreading as that of any news event until that time, and involvement in mourning and the funeral saturated the nation. This was thanks in part to use of the new telegraph, but newspapers, too, were perhaps at the zenith of their influence upon Americans and American life during the Civil War and post-war period. News syndicates were furnishing news of national importance to small-town papers. Great journalistic names abounded. A highly personal editorial style, high visibility, and forays into social reform and politics made national figures of such newspapermen as James Gordon Bennett and Horace Greeley.

Bennett's New York *Herald*, a penny paper, provided comprehensive if sometimes sensational coverage of the Civil War, with sixty-three correspondents in the field.

In 1871, George Jones's exposé of William Marcy "Boss" Tweed of New York in the New York *Times* led to the arrest and jailing of the latter, who had seized control of the municipal treasury and plundered it through faked leases, kickbacks, padded bills, phony vouchers, and a variety of quite modern aids for bilking the public.

Not all of the "fourth estate" watchdogs were in the East by any means: an exposé by the St. Louis Democrat uncovered the Whiskey Plot, a conspiracy of revenue officials with distillers to defraud the government of liquor taxes.

Another long depression hit between 1873 and 1896, and saw a wave of bank and business failures. As a solution to panic in 1873, the federal government released some $26 million in greenbacks. Overall, it was a period, however, of daring, personal pizzazz, enterprise, and exploitation. It was a time of the great inventors, as well as the robber barons of industry and the railroads. During the final quarter of the nineteenth century not only were the telephone, the automobile and the electric light invented, but also the typewriter, machinery for sewing shoes and other sewing machines, the linotype printer, the hand-held camera, the electric welder, the diesel engine, and dozens of other work enablers and conveniences.

Growing unemployment during the winter of 1893–94 brought groups of jobless men, under the leadership of populist Jacob Coxey of Ohio, on the march to Washington. Thousands demanded relief, a public works program, and an increase in the amount of money in circulation. Working conditions for those who had jobs, including women and children, were for the most part unspeakably bad in mines and factories; work, health, and safety laws would not come until after the turn of the century.

The Spanish-American War, a senseless episode of cloak-and-dagger diplomacy coupled with colonialist bravura and slogans (Remember the Maine!) pretty well rounded out the nineteenth century. Taken all in all, we had what was probably for most White, majority-culture Americans (especially in retrospect) the most peaceful, uneventful period in our history between the end of Reconstruction—about 1877—and the beginning of the First World War. The Black slaves, freed of legal slavery, but still of uncertain status as Americans and tied to the land by poverty and illiteracy; the Indians, vanquished, dying out in misery: these were indeed the silent minorities in a nation full of prosperous main streets and upward striving cities, and farms. White Americans were reasonably comfortable and contented.

The first years of the twentieth century—at least in many places and on the surface—were pretty much hangovers from the former century. People had a sense of belonging to wherever they were. If you were a New Englander, a Midwesterner, a hardworking homesteader of the Southwest, you were inclined to stay put for your lifetime, and expected your children to do the same. There was, enduringly, an inborn distrust by farmers and small-town people of city folk, Eastern money men, most foreigners, and the railroads.

Small wonder that the Sherman Anti-Trust Act was passed in 1890. The Pure Food and Drug Act of 1906 sought to prevent such delights for people as weevils in their flour. In 1903, a group of writers who were called the Muckrakers began to inveigh against and expose corruption in politics and certain aspects of social injustice, but it did not strike anyone as unusual that most Black children, not only in rural areas where they shared this lack with White children, but in small northern cities like Orange, New Jersey, did not own a pair of shoes.

After the successful flight by the Wright brothers at Kitty Hawk in 1903, aviation progressed quickly. Aviators trained at Love Field in Texas in 1917 and 1918 flew overseas in World War I; airmail service was inaugurated between New York and Washington, and the first transcontinental flight took place in 1920.

The century literally began with a bang when President McKinley was shot by an anarchist in 1901, but the great story of the first decade was the immigration into the United States of millions of working-class people, most of them farmers and laborers from Italy, Austria, and Russia. They had been preceded into this country by millions from Germany, Ireland, and Scandinavia in the years between 1840 and the 1880s—all of them voluntary immigrants in contrast to the Blacks from African coastal communities, and the Chinese, who had been brought here earlier to work on the plantations and the railroads.

But nothing even approached the immigration of the years between 1900 and 1910, during which period more than eight million people from Europe alone entered at the East Coast of the U.S. to become citizens. This was nearly half as many people as had immigrated to this country in all the years between 1820 and 1900. Then, during the four years following World War I, nearly four million more came, so that by 1920, a nation of some 76,000,000 had become a nation of nearly 106,000,000.

World War I was the sharp dividing line between the new century and the old. With it, the nostalgic image of America as a land apart came to an end. The Russian Revolution, erupting in the midst of the World War, helped to sweep away the last of the nineteenth century. America entered the war in 1917, turned the tide among the battleweary who had fought for three years, and Armistice was declared in 1918.

The war was over, but the world was changed. Two Europeans, essentially men of the nineteenth century, gave their names to key new words: Karl Marx, who died before the century even began, and Sigmund Freud, who published most of his studies after it started. Changes they had envisioned began to take place in post-war America. Not only the old taboos, but the old absolutes began to slip away. Patterns of class, family organization, and social behavior began breaking up.

The Volstead Act—The National Prohibition Enforcement Act—was made law in January 1920. By banning the legal sale of liquor, it made drinking seem more attractive to many who had never had much to do with it—including women. Further, it caused widespread flouting of law, for the first time, by otherwise responsible and respectable people. It gave rise to criminal activity, organized close to the surface of society, and condoned by a large part of the citizenry. It was, in short, an action by government-under-pressure that did long-lasting harm to the American people. Another post-war event with far-reaching implications for society was the Scopes Monkey Trial in Tennessee in 1925 which threw into question the origin of man, and to many, the existence of God himself.

The first radio station went on the air in 1920, and the first major radio network, NBC, was formed in 1926. So strong was the post-war suspicion of foreign influences, of radical thinking and possible anarchy, that two Italian workmen, Sacco and Vanzetti, whose ideas were considered "dangerous" were convicted on slim evidence of the murder of a night watchman in 1920, and put to death amid national and international furor in 1927.

In 1929, the Wall Street Crash brought the Roaring Twenties to a grinding halt. The world-wide Great Depression had begun. A veterans' bonus march, quite reminiscent of Coxey's Army, was met with armed troops by President Herbert Hoover. Families who were wiped out, and turned out of their homes, made do in many cases with shanties constructed from boxes and mashed tin cans in such areas as the marshy garbage dumps of the New Jersey meadows. Long, silent lines of men marched, gaunt with hunger, through the streets, and many froze to death in doorways and on park benches during the long, cold winters of the early thirties.

Economic ruin and disillusionment split the electorate in 1932. Not only did the Republicans and Democrats enter candidates, but also the Socialist Party, the Socialist Labor Party, the Communist Party, the Prohibition Party, the Farmer-Labor Party, and the Liberal Party. Franklin Delano Roosevelt won the presidency with 27,821,857 popular votes, and remained President of the United States through the next thirteen traumatic years. Serving longer than any President ever had, or probably ever will again, he was the only President that people born in the late twenties can remember being there throughout their childhood and early adolescence.

Thousands of banks had failed by the eve of Roosevelt's inauguration (then held in March). Virtually every bank still in business closed its doors or restricted its operations. Roosevelt declared a bank holiday, and took immediate steps to provide some measure of economic stability. He called a special session of the 73rd Congress on March 9: by the time it had ended in June (the famous hundred days) it had enacted comprehensive legislation concerning banks and protection of deposits; industry; employment; labor; and agriculture—all aimed at relief and recovery. Between that time and the end of the President's first term, dozens of pieces of social legislation were put into effect to revitalize the country and provide a new awareness, as well as a new vocabulary, for Americans. Among them were the Works Progress Administration (WPA); the Rural Electrification Act; the Soil Conservation Act; the Social Security Act; the National Labor Relations Act; and the Revenue Taxes, which taxed big business, and the incomes of the rich, more rigorously. Thus were the needs of the jobless, the rural poor, the aged and those suffering from unfair employment practices made matters of public concern and public policy.

Many of our "watchdog" commissions were brought

into being during this period, including the Securities and Exchange Commission and the Federal Communications Commission. Mr. Roosevelt, who early on used radio to explain and gain public consent for his policies, fully understood the potential power and political implications of the mass medium, radio, and how important it was that its entrepreneurs be subject to regulation on behalf of the people.

In 1934, the hearings of the Senate Munitions Investigating Committee brought to light the heavy profits made by munitions manufacturers during World War I. They set the stage not only for the neutrality legislation of 1935 and 1937, but for the isolationism that made Americans turn a deaf ear to those who warned of Hitler's "Gathering Storm." An estimated 6,000,000 Jewish men, women, and children—no one will ever really know how many—were to die in extermination camps and as the result of inhuman pseudo-scientific experiments, neighborhood raids and other devices of government-by-madmen between the time Hitler came to power with his street ruffian troops in the early thirties, and the destruction of the Third Reich, in 1945.

For most families, the Depression continued throughout the thirties. As late as 1939, a Food Stamp Plan—primarily launched to dispose of surplus agricultural products to persons on relief—was inaugurated in Rochester, New York, and later in more than 100 other cities. It was discontinued due to America's involvement in the War. Throughout the late thirties and early forties, fear of subversives and aliens was strong, and indeed organizations such as the German-American Bund held shouting, quasi-military meetings, turned out in Madison Square Garden thousands strong. All this led to the Alien Registration Act of 1940 which permitted (required, in fact) fingerprinting of aliens and laid out strict rules for their admission and deportation. The act made it unlawful to teach or advocate the overthrow or the destruction of the United States by force or violence, or to be a member of any group which so advocated.

World War II began, formally, with the declaration of War by France and Great Britain, and the crushing of Poland. British and French troops retreated and were trapped on the coast of France by the triumphant march of Hitler's armies through the Netherlands and Belgium; they were evacuated from Dunkirk during the last week in May and early June of 1940 in 861 small pleasure craft and fishing boats. Altogether 338,226 men escaped across the channel to England, and France fell. The Battle of Britain, during which Hitler tried to conquer the British with heavy air raids, lasted from August through October of that year.

By this time, the Neutrality Acts had been amended—thanks mainly to the leadership of President Roosevelt—to permit so-called "lend-lease" arms aid to Britain in 1941. President Roosevelt, elected for the unprecedented third term in 1940, was a firm hand at the helm. Very much the wartime leader, as he had been stabilizer of the economy in the Depression, he enunciated the Four Freedoms—which were reaffirmations, really, of the Bill of Rights: freedom of speech and expression; freedom from want; freedom from fear; and freedom of worship. America, under his leadership, spoke poignantly to the oppressed and frightened and was ready, psychologically at least, to enter the war on the side of the Allies against Germany, Italy, and their hangers-on in Europe when the Japanese attacked Pearl Harbor in Hawaii, in December of 1941.

Through 1942 and 1943 America fought both in Europe and Asia. There were some serious defeats, but Americans on the home front worked hard to support the war. By early 1943 there were 27 million workers frozen into war jobs. They encountered some new experiences, some of them foreshadowing the future. There were, for instance, terrible race riots in Detroit in June of 1941, brought about by the treatment of rural Blacks from the South who had come North to work in war plants. A Fair Employment Practices Committee was established to curb discrimination, and non-discrimination clauses were written into war contracts, but a Fair Employment Practices Law was defeated three successive times in 1946, 1950, and 1952 before it was finally passed by Congress into law.

Rationing began with automobile tires in December 1941, to be followed by coupon books for sugar and coffee, and separate books for gasoline and fuel oil. The Emergency Price Control Act was passed in 1942, and the Office of Price Administration fixed ceiling prices for all commodities and rents. Point rationing started early in 1943 with meat, fats, butter, and, later, shoes. At the peak, there were thirteen different rationing programs.

Millions of paperbound books in special Armed Forces Editions were distributed to service men in all the war theaters. They were the first books that many of them had ever had; some were unable to read them comfortably because of their functional illiteracy. The Office of War Information and the Office of Strategic Services began information and counterintelligence activity in June 1942. The development of the atomic bomb began that same year under a veil of deepest secrecy. In the United Nations Declaration, twenty-six nations vowed not to make a separate peace with either Germany or Japan.

The big event of 1944 was the landing of the Allied Armies on the coast of France on "D" Day—June 6, 1944, under the leadership of American General Dwight D. Eisenhower. Planning for post-war reconstruction began, and preliminary drafting of a charter for a world-wide organization to maintain peace and security in the world. Most significant for its long-term implications, the GI Bill of Rights (GI was the slang term for American servicemen, meaning Government Issue) was signed, authorizing educational and other benefits for men who had fought in the war. It was one of the most brilliant and far-reaching moves ever made by any government.

Capitulation of Germany came in May 1945, a month after the death of President Roosevelt. In June, Germany was placed under an Allied Control Council—with the U.S.S.R. as one of the controllers—and divided into four occupation zones; in retrospect, probably this ranks as one of the most unstrategic moves ever made.

In August, the first atomic bomb was used against Japan, and the Japanese surrendered. The United Nations Charter went into effect in October, and an immense relief, reconstruction, and recovery program went into action under UN auspices (UNRRA) and later through the United States' own Marshall Plan.

The days long anticipated had arrived! Consolidation, security, were uppermost in the minds of American people. The Depression was over, the war was over! At last, they could begin to live, to do what they wanted to do, to buy all the things denied for so long and now made more desirable by wartime research and development of new materials and methods. They were willing—eager—to give billions in foreign aid, for economic assistance to Europe and other underdeveloped areas of the world, if only they could just not be bothered any more about anybody's troubles.

The "cold war" atmosphere pervaded the country, and defense spending sustained the economy. Internal loyalty checks in our own departments of government led to such dramas as that of the accusation of long-time State Department expert Alger Hiss, by a former Communist courier. In 1950, espionage trials of those allegedly involved in atomic spying on behalf of the Russians led to the conviction and execution of an American couple, the Rosenbergs, on spy charges.

Meanwhile, despite the shadow of the Bomb, America felt good about the future. Families, homes and careers were energetically rebuilt between 1946 and 1950, during which half decade the population jumped by close to 11 million, to 151,400,000. By the end of the 1950s, it had risen to some 179,300,000. During 1967, we passed the 200,000,000 mark, for a total post-World War II increase of over 40 per cent.

The great forces set in motion by the war, which were to create the immense social changes of the sixties and onward, were not fully grasped in the first euphoric post-war years. The huge migration of hundreds of thousands of unskilled, illiterate agriculture workers—from farms in the

South to the industrial cities of the Northeast, Midwest, and West Coast—was not, somehow, understood as the cause of radical, permanent change in our society. Neither, at first, was the extensive and purposeful investment in scientific research and technological development during the war years, which was vastly stepped up after the war ended.

Additions to recorded knowledge were generally haphazard prior to the twentieth century, the product of individual curiosity and discovery rather than the systematic, well-supported efforts of government and industry. World War II changed this pattern in a revolutionary way. To quote Dan Lacy, sociologist, writer, and publisher, and the man who, in my opinion, has most clearly expressed the devastating results in human and social terms: "the demonstrated results of applying massive research and development funds to the achievement of predetermined objectives were overwhelming, and reached their dramatic climax with the explosion of the atomic bomb. Paced by government programs in the fields of defense and space exploration, the society as a whole devoted enormous sums in the post-war decades to scientific research and technological development. Fifteen billions of dollars was an average annual investment for these purposes. This was more than the entire gross national product of all but a few nations, and more than that of the U.S. itself until a few decades ago. For the first time in the history of the world, a nation deliberately mobilized all of its relevant resources to achieve a radical and comprehensive technological innovation as rapidly as possible."

There was an immediate impact on the economy deriving from this effort. To continue to quote Mr. Lacy:

"Most of billions of dollars spent have gone . . . into development, or the immediate application of the results of research to practical economic life. A new chemical with special properties is scarcely discovered before it is widely marketed as a herbicide, quickly displacing thousands of laborers from their task of chopping weeds. The principles of the digital computer are devised, and within a decade hundreds of thousands of men and women are at work making, servicing, programming, and using them . . ."

In the name of progress, the technologists gave little thought to the social dislocations, the human costs, the varied prices that people would pay for the kind of society that was being created. Apparently, and unfortunately, the social scientists—the health, education, and other planners —gave little thought to them either—until too late.

By 1950, one of the great social change agents of all time had begun to appear in people's homes: television. The first TV signals had been transmitted in 1927, and fully commercial television was inaugurated in 1941, but its development for general transmission had to wait until the war was over. By 1952 it was estimated that 8 million TV sets were in use, and more than 60 million people were able to see the political conventions, and the candidates, in the 1952 presidential elections.

In 1950, the American people received a terribly traumatic shock: war was not over for them, and world responsibilities would continue to impinge. In June, North Korean forces, equipped with Soviet-made weapons, invaded South Korea. And where *was* South Korea? It was a republic created with the aid of the United States in 1948, a partitioning-off of the non-Communist portion of an Asian country which had figured in the Sino-Japanese War of the thirties. (The United States was in a partitioning mood in 1948, dividing up countries and land areas between contending parties: that same year, Palestine was partitioned—by mandate of the United Nations, but with heavy U.S. influence—to provide, at last, a homeland, Israel, for the Jewish refugees who swarmed, homeless, through Europe.)

Americans had to look at their atlases to find South Korea, but nearly 25,000 American soldiers were killed there in the UN-sponsored "police action" and more than 100,000 were wounded or missing in action. Safety, security and wartime leadership ability were elected to the presidency in 1952, in the person of General Eisenhower, hero of World War II victories.

The social, political, and intellectual climate of the early 1950s was characterized by widespread distrust of scholars and other so-called "eggheads"; the initial belief that computer technology and electronic communications would make books—and print in general—obsolete; suspicion of political and ethnic differences; and the lack of involvement of people generally in social problems. People seemed to be tired of thinking, of planning; they wanted to play, to be entertained, and not to work so hard at just living as they had during the Depression and the war. Educational excellence at any level was rare, and equal educational opportunity for all children even rarer. The "cold war" psychology led the United States to turn in upon itself, to give more attention to preservation of the so-called "American way of life."

Television egged people on. It told them what they wanted to hear because this was good for sales. In more and more homes it showed a stylized version of what was known as "the good life" everyone was supposed to have, or hope for. Conformity was the social ideal, and "togetherness" the byword. Writers, actors, and directors who represented alternative life styles or politically unpopular points of view were "blacklisted" and hounded out of jobs, and sometimes literally to death. For the huge generation of children born in the late 1940s and growing up in the '50s, the TV set was often the first friend, and the family's most prized possession. It provided baby-sitting service, spectator sport, and a vision of what the world should be like. It told us how we should feel about marriage, as well as the kitchen floor. Its ads told us what to want, and that we already deserved more and knew better about almost everything than our parents, or any previous authority.

The stage was set for the career of Joseph McCarthy, a senator from Wisconsin, who, with the aid of television, fanned the fears and suspicions of the American people while conducting investigations of alleged Communists—often synonymous, in his mind, with any individuals who were suspected of "deviant" thinking or libertarian ideas.

Intellectual freedom dropped to a new low during this period, and President Eisenhower himself appealed to the nation "not to join the book burners." The horrors of Nazi Germany, where on May 10, 1933, some 25,000 books with ideas the Nazis did not care for were burned, were called to mind.

Actually, from the perspective of some twenty years later this wave of anti-intellectualism in the 1950s probably paved the way in the political arena for the renewed interest in books and magazines, the new respect for their importance which was to follow, by spotlighting them as purveyors of ideas—popular and unpopular—and emphasizing their potency instead of their innocence and blandness. But in the early 1950s, identity as a reader was not desirable, and few young people wanted to be thought of as readers. There were almost no bookshelves, or books, in the nuclear households, and no grandmothers to read aloud or tell stories. Extended families were not part of the white, middle-class, suburban image to which so many aspired, and with depression and wartime conditions over, it was no longer necessary for several generations to live together.

Many people by the '50s had already begun to feel uneasy, even threatened, by technology, as their lives and jobs were increasingly affected by its applications. Wry signs appeared in factories and offices reminding workers that "you can be replaced by a computer."

Meanwhile, the mass of poor rural people who had flocked to jobs in the cities were still there—many now without jobs, or the skills to compete for them in the increasingly technology-oriented market. Middle-class White families headed for the suburbs and left behind them the public institutions which their taxes had supported: the schools, the hospitals, the police forces, the fire departments, and the libraries. Although on the edge of financial collapse, these agencies were still expected to serve more citizens than ever—the new "inner city" dwellers who needed help desperately but often did not know where to find it, or how to ask for or use it. Nor did they produce enough tax revenues to support the institutions.

By the end of the 1950s, raised expectations, frustration, and total unpreparedness for change had sown the seeds of social upheaval throughout an apparently bland decade. Millions of excluded people—excluded from the good life and the products shown on TV, unable to get jobs that required literacy and skills they did not possess—appeared in the dark corners of society where they had existed, all but invisible, for so long. They appeared to demand their human, civil, social, economic, and educational rights—rights which depended, more often than not—on access to information and knowledge, and help in applying it to their own lives.

During this same post-war period, the American educational system—in reality thousands of separate systems—began to show unmistakable signs of long neglect and undernourishment. Fathers who had had a chance at education through the GI Bill, and had helped to bring higher education back up to snuff with their earnestness and desire to learn, began to look hard at the elementary and secondary schools their taxes paid for. During the 1950s, several pieces of legislation, and at least one Supreme Court decision, responded to the sad state into which American education had fallen, and paved the way for improvement.

Of abiding significance in terms of both social change and educational development was the Supreme Court decision of 1954 that the "separate but equal" schools to which Black children had been relegated in the South since Reconstruction were inherently *unequal*, and that segregation was deeply damaging to Black children. Although more than twenty years later, integrated and fully equal educational opportunity for children of all ethnic backgrounds and all social and economic levels is still far from reality in most communities in both North and South, the Court's decision and its aftermath focused the attention of parents and the power structures alike on the terrible and far-reaching effects of limited learning opportunity.

In 1956, after years of effort, the first federal legislation authorizing funds for the support of public libraries was passed. It provided pitifully small sums of money to states to begin library services in rural areas which had none, but it was a start. In 1958, after the launching of Sputnik by the Soviet Union, the U. S. Congress passed a landmark piece of legislation on behalf of educational revival in America: the National Defense Education Act. Born of panic because the United States had been preceded into space exploration by its political and scientific rival, the act provided funds in areas that were relevant and most sorely lacking in most elementary and secondary schools: science, mathematics, and modern foreign languages. At a later date, reading was among the subjects added for special attention.

Education of the tremendous new generation of Americans had begun at last to be seen as a national responsibility, at least in part. By the end of the '50s, one out of five American families moved every year, and a large percentage, cutting across class and economic lines, several times in each decade. In this context, the inequalities among thousands of disparate school systems became a glaring problem that could no longer be brushed aside.

Related, inextricably, to all of the foregoing, was the development of the Civil Rights Movement, which began as a demand by Black people for their human rights, and escalated—and is still escalating—into a demand for a genuinely pluralistic society, and for equality and recognition by all minorities and oppressed segments of society.

In December 1955, a year after the Supreme Court decision regarding segregated schools, a tired Black woman going home from work on the bus in Montgomery, Alabama, struck the spark that lighted the waiting tinder, and began the most far-reaching reality of our century. Mrs. Rosa Parks took a seat in the front of the bus in which she was riding. She knew all too well that Black people were supposed to sit in the back, but the front was where an empty seat was. She sat in it, refused the command to move and was arrested. The bus boycott by the Black community of Montgomery which followed established Dr. Martin Luther King, Jr., as the leader of the non-violent resistance movement to attain justice for Black people.

With unerring sense that education was—and is—the most essential, over the long term, of all the rights they would fight for, Black leadership stood behind the right of a young Black woman to enter the University of Alabama the following year. In 1957, federal troops were ordered by President Eisenhower to Little Rock, Arkansas, to achieve integration of Central High School.

With the advent of the 1960s, the pace of the Civil Rights Movement quickened, with sit-ins, freedom rides, and some vicious murders. Civil Rights leaders led thousands of minority groups people, and White sympathizers, in a march on Washington, to dramatize needs and express dissatisfactions, in 1963. The murder of John F. Kennedy, the hope-inspiring, charismatic young President who followed Eisenhower and tried to turn the nation's attention toward its towering domestic problems, probably helped to gain acceptance of some of the most wide-ranging domestic social legislation the country had yet seen.

In Lyndon B. Johnson, vice-presidential heir to a year of unexpired term in the presidential office, the United States had a skillful, canny politician who knew how to use every advantage. He rode hard upon the country's sensitivity and sense of guilt to launch, and get passed into law, a great collection of civil-rights and educational programs that addressed the needs of the poor, the minorities, the decaying cities, and the desperation in the rural areas. Elected in his own right in 1964, President Johnson, proud of his early role as a teacher, established the responsibility of the federal government in assuring educational opportunity to all children, regardless of their local tax base.

The War on Poverty did not eliminate poverty as some fuzzy-minded and not very bright idealists had apparently thought it might, nor was its success visible or measurable in exactly the way in which some thought it would be. But its effects were far-reaching, and continue to be significant, and its real successes will not be apparent for many years to come. For poor and minority people themselves, the programs—community action, Head Start, legal services, Job Corps, and countless others—provided some exposure to potential, a taste of leadership, a sampling of self-determination. But public opinion and politics were fickle and interest short-lived. Overly high expectations, and too little fulfillment brought frustration. Riots and cries of "Burn, Baby, Burn," filled the ghettos, and fear swept the country in the late '60s. Senator Robert Kennedy, civil-rights advocate, brother of the slain President, and contender for the presidency in 1968, and Dr. Martin Luther King, Jr., spiritual as well as political leader of Black rebellion, were both assassinated. People who had once been without hope were now resentful of the snail's pace of social justice within the law, and the people who had never wanted them to have it anyway saw their chance to fight back.

The War on Poverty and the other Great Society programs of the Johnson years had some effects on middle-class White Americans as well. For the young people coming of age out of the baby boom of the '40s, the Civil Rights Movement became the Human Rights Movement, the chance to affirm individuality and personhood. Attending, graduating from college in unprecedented numbers, their favorite word was NOW. Inspired and excited by the rebellion around them, revolted by the plastic materialism of the times, they took up the fight.

After experimenting with carrying what they took to be the detachment of their elders to its extreme by immersing themselves in a bath of emotion and symbols of total rejection, they seemed, as a generation, to do an about-face which featured involvement and deep commitment to human values. To the thousands of young Americans working at home in the VISTA program, and other community programs among the poor and oppressed, and abroad in underdeveloped countries in the Peace Corps, America began to be perceived as a truly multi-cultural, multi-ethnic society, and the world as a place full of friends rather than enemies.

It was the young people who rejected first the narrow vision of "people proof" machines, and the theory that whatever was newest and biggest, was best. The generation that had been brought up on thousands of hours of television rejected the notion that one medium replaces another, and elected to be, do, see, listen to, create and think its own thing. In such an atmosphere, books took on a new life, along with camera, transistor radio, tape recorder, TV set and hi-fi, as supporters of a highly individualistic life style.

Even more exciting, as the decade of the '60s unfurled, the idealism, the new insights and objectives, the concern, the humanism and the daring of the young caught the imagination of their elders, who came within a short span of years to admire and emulate them. Perhaps the generation gap, subject of anxiety for only a few years, was so quickly closed because the latent power of education was rekindled and was paying off. The GI Bill of Rights provided an education beyond the high school level for a whole generation of young men—the same young men who were exposed to books and reading through the wartime distribution of paperbacks—and who were now the fathers of young Americans in the '60s. Perhaps education was the reason that parents caught up with the generation gap so quickly.

As the twentieth century advanced into the 1970s, rebellion against the tyranny of technology began to spread. Privacy, or the lack of it, became more of an issue, as computers delved ever more deeply into people's lives. The poisonous influence of the Vietnam war shook the confidence of Americans in their leaders, destroyed national self-esteem. Nightly television scenes of death and suffering hardened many Americans, especially the young, and caused them to lose their ability to feel or care. The courageous fight for rights too often lapsed, in deep depression, into license. A frightening plague of drugs, with accompanying crimes of violence, swept over the country as old certainties and values seemed totally lost.

Again, it was the young people whose awareness of the insidiousness of the Vietnam war, and their resentment of the way it was brutalizing and sapping away money and attention that was badly needed elsewhere, finally galvanized the forces that brought America's involvement to an end, many years too late.

Richard Nixon, who had been Vice-President under Dwight Eisenhower, became the nation's President in 1968, elected largely on promises that he would end the Vietnam war. Instead of doing this, he escalated the war, and tried to reverse, or financially starve to death, most of the educational and social programs that had been established. A second term won, Americans learned later, by the use of bribes, lies, and "dirty tricks," ended in disaster in a tangle of deceit and criminal charges as Nixon resigned just short of the impeachment proceedings which had been agreed upon by the Congress. He had, finally, withdrawn American troops from Asia, but the American people were left in the middle seventies, with mounting inflation, deepening economic depression, and a deepening spiritual depression as well.

As the country approached the start of its Bicentennial observance, the more than 220,000,000 people of the United States were a people trying to recover hope and confidence. They were people sated with speed and noise, and alert at last to the dangers of bigness, of greed, and the stultifying effects of the banal, the transitory. They were suspicious of the power elite—whoever it may be—and the closed society; the "zero defect" psychology, with its negation of human values and processes.

We Americans have, in the recent past, faced up to problems we did not even know were going to exist twenty-five years ago: pollution, congestion, racial violence, polarization of races and classes; crime that has reached an intolerable level; the disappearance of energy resources; international distrust, even hatred; drugs and the dissolution of traditional values and absolutes—with no guidelines to replace them. Modesty, moderation, and reticence seem to have vanished totally, and the personal landscapes of many people seem to be littered with broken connections with family, religion, community, country, and self.

How can we come out of it? Will we be able to recover stability, belief in the future, self-confidence, even some measure of joy?

There are hopeful signs. There are indicators of a new sense of reality, a new respect for living one day at a time, and making the most of it. We have learned that it is easy to give answers, but hard to ask the right questions. We have learned that freedom calls for discipline, and that form has value. We have learned that sequence has some uses as does the kind of order that is imposed upon ourselves, from within. Yet, there is little tolerance for discomfort or inconvenience; what would we do if faced with real hardship?

The nineteenth-century "melting-pot" is definitely gone, and young and old are discovering, or holding proudly to, their own cultural heritage. Few feel self-conscious about being "different" from the rest of the crowd, or obliged to live in a way that does not suit them. People want aspirations, educations and life-styles that fit them, that are tailored to their own dimensions, with room to grow and ease of alteration if desired.

Deeply held convictions and a worked-out code of ethics are coming back in style. The yearning for privacy, for individuality and the means of expressing it seems to have grown as people reject herding. Also, the value of words has begun to revive. As people spread out in their lives, and in their minds, the struggle to preserve choices and alternatives imbues with new value the right of inquiry, and the free flow of knowledge.

In such a landscape, the potential need for access to information and knowledge seems clear. There is need for cultural materials and programs to affirm and give pride in identity; help in coping with survival problems; help with a term paper; help in writing a poem; help in retraining for a new job; or simply in becoming a more assured, articulate person.

Where can Americans turn to find the personal reinforcement, the intellectual agility, the communication skills, the economic flexibility they must have in the complex society ours has become?

Libraries—cultural, learning, resource, or information centers—but libraries all the same: libraries *can be* the answer. Inadequately equipped, unprepared, though many of them are at present to fulfill the roles into which destiny has pushed them, they are the only agencies on the horizon with any chance of being able, successfully, to do the job.

Chapter II: The Need to Know and Library Response

Aristotle told us, long ago, that "men by nature desire to know." But is it true to any great extent, one wonders, even for people who are unaware of how much there is to know, and how it affects their lives? Conversely, can there be such a thing as more to know than people can sort out, or see any use for—so that knowledge becomes an out-of-focus blur, something annoying to be tuned out? These are, perhaps, pertinent questions for our time, especially for our society.

Insofar as it is a human, universal need, the need to know is shaped by many factors. It derives only in part from awareness of the knowledge universe. It depends in some degree upon the level of intelligence, and the amount of training one has had in the arts of inquiry and relationship—often, but not always, inculcated or heightened by formal education. More important, it springs from an individual's awareness of the world around him, and his degree of sensitivity to those who share it with him. Perhaps most of all, the need to know is related to one's self-image, to his sense of *mattering*—that which empowers him to believe that once he is knowledgeable, his response to information, to the onrush of events, will have some meaning.

In general it can be said that exposure to knowledge whets the appetite for more; but unless the exposure has some structure, some order and provides for an assimilation/application process, mental indigestion, followed by tune-out, can occur.

Remembered experience spawns the need to know. It dictates the demand for choices, the desire to know what one is getting into, to look before leaping and to resist when necessary. It is assimilated knowledge—much of which has become wisdom—that enables a single person, or a whole race of people to resist, to stand fast against a tide by which they do not want to be submerged, and to survive against impossible odds. This is true, for example, of Indian, Black, and other minority people, for this is what they have done when faced with the values, the priorities, and the power of an alien, majority, culture.

Many people would in fact like to know things that they do not dream of knowing. The need to know can be developed, nurtured, expanded. Motivation to know, to find out, can most easily be encouraged in children, but it is never too late. With care, and patient effort, the need to know, the desire to learn, can be developed in young adults, and with increasing difficulty, in older adults.

Motivation is composed of *expectations* and *interests*. There are self-expectations; the expectations one believes that others have of him (family, teachers, peers); and the expectations that one has of others, of events, of the future. Self-expectation is deeply rooted in self-esteem. A poor self-identity, lack of esteem for self, too often colors, and is reflected back, in the esteem and expectation others have of oneself: parents, neighbors, teachers, and others in authority. Occasionally, low self-esteem and expectation can be mitigated, even reversed, by someone who refuses to accept a child's (or even an adult's) negative self-view, and helps him begin to revise it. Literature, and the case histories of sociology and psychology, are full of instances in which because someone "believed in them" people have developed the positive self-image that provides the foundation for the desire to know.

Interests and concerns are the other part of the equation.

Interests are both internal and external—the internal ones centered on self, the emotions and concerns. Does anyone love me? Am I even worthy of being loved? Will my fears come true? These are all matters of burning interest to every human being. External interests require time to ferment and space in the mind, and if possible, in the surroundings, to spread them out and examine them. Interest development requires stimulation but also some solitude. Interests need cultivating and pruning, like weeds and flowers running wild in a garden.

The scope of people's interests is immense, and goes far beyond the here and now of their own lives. They are more than skin deep, and do not relate only to what one knows about or has actually seen. Interests in an imaginary world are not mutually exclusive with those of the so-called real world. People—young people especially—like to know about things and people as they are, but also as they could, or might, be. They want to know about themselves, but they can learn to want to know about the people around them. They are susceptible, too, to interest in times, places, and people far removed from their own experience. An interesting manifestation of this is the gang names often used by the young people of the city ghettos: Black, Puerto Rican, and other limited-experience youngsters become the Lords, the Dragons, or the Knights.

Imaginations must be inflamed, for trained imaginations are the tools of problem-solving, of extrapolation, of invention. Few parents—or other adult models who influence children—seem to make the effort to bring a selection of images into focus for them, probably because they do not even think of it, or perhaps because they do not know how. Ability to relate one idea to another is vital.

Interest development requires that a child—or an adult, for that matter—receive large doses of attention from a person with whom he not only communicates, but feels a sense of communion. Mother, father, friend, grandfather, social worker, neighbor, parole officer—it does not matter what the formal relationship is, as long as a real relationship exists, and that the person feels known and liked —valued—believed in—by someone who envisions for him things that he cannot envision for himself, has not yet learned to expect of himself.

Interests are first formulated, then identified, and later expressed. When they come to the point of being expressed, they enter the stream of communications: they can be talked about, listened to about, looked at, drawn, written and read. The expectation and the interest combine to motivate the knower in his seeking to know.

The urge to become a reader—a knower—is complex and internalized. It is tied up with being able to see oneself as being, becoming, doing, mattering. It is related to the desire to test the present, the belief that there will be a future, and that one will be a part of it. Nurturing the need to know, and the degree of expectation and interest which leads to reading, listening, viewing, is not easy in a climate of crisis. Children, even young ones, learn to turn off and tune out much that assails them, and so to preserve something of themselves and their privacy. They learn to protect themselves, insofar as possible, by not learning to want knowledge they think is not for them.

In summary, then, exposure and access to books and other sources of knowledge and information make a difference; people links, people to bridge the gap between oneself and sources of knowledge, make a difference; and self-esteem and positive self-image, are at once motivators to know, and are generated and reinforced by knowing.

Once born, the need to know is satisfied in several kinds of ways. Much depends upon how close one is to the source of knowledge; how complex the information is; how much one believes he needs to know about it; and whether one can interpret it for himself, or needs the help of others.

The primitive, like the small child, finds out through firsthand experience what he needs to know. He looks, smells, feels, tastes, and listens, and interprets his findings in light of his own limited experience, according to his need. At a more advanced stage, he uses words to symbolize his query and his need, and *asks*. The simple man in a simple society tests his own observation and interpretation against those of his immediate circle.

Those who are further removed from the source of direct or firsthand information about what they need to know, rely on secondary sources—including the experience and the interpretations of those long dead—to help them know, understand, process, recycle, and use the complex information they receive.

These are the people who, through thousands of years, have used libraries. For many ages now, reading has been the most sophisticated means of feeding interest, and of finding out. Precision of thought and expression of thought have demanded language; manipulation of written language has been the central skill that enabled the knower—or the would-be knower—to analyze, interpret, and apply the knowledge he received in any form.

Society is now in the process of clarifying and expanding the uses of literacy, even the definition of literacy. Although many needs to know are now met by sound and picture forms of communication, the major social, economic, and political business of the day is still carried out by those who characteristically use *reading* skills in all their acts of communication. Conciseness and clarity, required to express ideas in writing, are essential also to the creative use of sight and sound symbols. Literacy skills apply to what is viewed and heard, as well as read.

All of the research results we have tell us that readers deal more effectively with the audio and visual media, as well as with problems, opportunities, and human relationships, than non-readers. Readers are better listeners, and more active participants in social enterprises, and reading is seen by today's young people around the world —not just in the United States—as a social, rather than an anti-social, activity.

Over the past two hundred years in America, as we have briefly recounted, we have seen the number of things to know multiply almost beyond belief. We have seen the rush of events, the applications of knowledge increasingly affect the everyday lives of all Americans. As society has become more complex, the ability to ask one's neighbor, or to test for oneself the meaning of events has diminished in usefulness. Minds are better trained, and in an increasingly interdependent society, Americans have found that they could not go their own way and let some one else take care of public matters, but must take some responsibility themselves.

Where then, did people get their information while America was growing up? Did the American people feel "the need to know" sufficiently to organize knowledge resources, and were there libraries for them to go to?

Libraries in America have been, from the start, a little bit different from the libraries that preceded them in the ancient and medieval worlds. The germ of a concept—that information and libraries were required equipment for people in a democracy—was built, implicitly, right into the constitution. The statesmen who imposed the pattern of their thought upon our early history, institutions, and national goals, were among the best-read men of their own or any other time: Jefferson, Adams, and Madison, and of course, Ben Franklin, whose affinity for books and for libraries is famous.

Such men envisioned, and in a sense mandated, the universal education that was to follow, and the eventual development of libraries that would be available to, and used by, all the people. But although the founding fathers gave libraries a big push toward their destiny by entrusting government to the common man—who would have to be informed to make it work—it has taken nearly two centuries fully to democratize library use in America.

The historic library ideal, imported from the Old World to the New, was that of a repository, a resource for scholars and the leisure class, the educated elite, who needed to draw upon the accumulated wisdom and experience of mankind. The papyrus rolls of Egypt, the clay tablets of Babylon and Assyria, were accessible to only a few scholars—the only few who could read them or make sense of their contents. Until the growth of libraries on American soil, librarians were fellow scholars who were expected to know, collect, and care for the books. Patrons of libraries were supposed to be knowledgeable about what they wanted, why they wanted it, and how to use it. It was the job of the librarian-scholars to see to it that what they sought was there, to help find it, and above all, to preserve it.

The strong ties between libraries, scholarship, and religion, reinforced by the retreat of manuscripts and the remnants of the intellectual life into the monasteries of the middle ages, lingered long and strong in early America. It was monks such as the sixth-century Benedictines who were required by their rule to read and study during a part of every day, who kept alive such culture and knowledge as survived. It was not until after the fifteenth-century invention of printing that any institution had enough books to have a special room, or a library, to house them. It was in the library of the Escorial that Philip II of Spain first arranged books in cases against the walls.

The Bay Psalm Book, first book published in the Colonies in 1640, was easily the best seller of the first Colonial century, having reached twenty-seven editions by 1750. A native literature began to develop almost at once: diaries and accounts of daily life and survival in the wilderness by such as William Bradford and John Winthrop; musings, with heavy religious overtones, on the nature and responsibilities of liberty; and apologias for such religious-political hysterias as the Salem witchcraft episodes. Jonathan Edwards, a Massachusetts clergyman, created some interest in freedom of the will. Cotton Mather, most prolific of the Colonial authors, published over four hundred works. Roger Williams, radical critic of the religious and political order, attacked the conservative ideas of Mather. And there was even a woman poet, Anne Bradstreet. More interesting for the adventure-minded were the first person accounts of Indian wars, life as an Indian captive—one of the most exciting by a Pennsylvania woman, Mrs. Mary Rowlandson—and journals by explorers and surveyors.

The Bray Parish libraries, founded by Dr. Thomas Bray,

co-founder also of the Society for the Propagation of the Gospel in Foreign Parts, appeared first in 1696 in Annapolis, and then in some thirty other Maryland parishes. Other free circulating libraries begun under Dr. Bray's aegis were in New York's Trinity Parish, and in Charleston, South Carolina, about 1699. The private library the great university library, began to flourish early in the Colonies. The library of Cotton Mather was said to have contained some three thousand volumes; John Harvard, an English clergyman who came to America in 1637, left his library and half of his estate—to which the Massachusetts General Court added a grant—to the new college at Cambridge. Henrico College, later The College of William and Mary, had a significant library early in the seventeenth century.

Altogether, nine colleges were founded in Colonial America before the Revolution, including, in addition to those already mentioned: Yale; Franklin's Academy (later to become the University of Pennsylvania); and those that became Princeton, Columbia, Brown, Rutgers, and Dartmouth. Nearly all had sectarian roots, and all were built around library collections.

Colonial Americans of a lower economic and social level were pretty fully occupied with clearing land, plowing, building, and just plain surviving during the early years to pay much attention to education and politics—two of the great stimuli to literature and libraries. The gentry, busy developing trade and commerce, needed to pay a little more attention to what was happening beyond their front doors. Massachusetts laws of 1642 and 1647 respectively imposed fines for the neglect of the education of the young, and required all towns of fifty families or more to provide a teacher for instruction in reading and writing. All towns of one hundred families or more were required to establish a Latin grammar school. (There was one in Boston as early as 1636.) The law made it optional whether the school would be tax-supported or fee-supported, and imposed a penalty for non-compliance.

Laws similar to the one in Massachusetts were passed in Connecticut and in New Hampshire within a short time.

Although historians disagree as to the extent of enforcement of these laws, evidence points to a higher level of literacy in New England than elsewhere. Parochial schools, private schools, and charity schools for poor children blossomed in New York and Pennsylvania, while in the southern colonies tutors and private schools educated the children of planters, and "pauper schools" and apprenticeships provided rudimentary training for the poor.

The development of libraries has been markedly related to the climate and concerns of the times, and tied to the development of educational opportunity in every period of our history. Libraries have been organized largely in terms of the institutions, individuals, or jurisdictions that were willing to support them.

In line with the scholarly tradition, the academic libraries came first—growing out of the private interests and generosities of educated benefactors, and supporting the highest level of education. Next came the small town and the city libraries, often directly related to the need of students and schools. School libraries, geared specifically to the use of students at the high school level, did not appear until, in the nineteenth century, high school education itself gradually became established as a norm. In 1827, Massachusetts became the first state to require that every town of five hundred families or more provide a high school.

The need of Americans to cope with choices and options led very early to some degree of popular support for libraries, in recognition of their role in education, in industrial development, and in the achievement of public and personal goals. It was essentially the event-filled, fast-moving society itself which began to transform a scholarly institution with an historic function and name into a public agency conceived to meet the information and knowledge needs of an increasingly restless, politically stimulated, voluble, educated, and expectant citizenry.

Boston, New York, Philadelphia, and Charleston were all well supplied with newspapers, which, during the early eighteenth century were increasingly critical of the government. In New York, John Peter Zenger, arrested in 1734 for articles in his *New York Weekly* inveighing against the provincial government, was acquitted in 1735 in the first successful victory for freedom of the press, and the free expression of ideas and political dissent.

It is no accident, but a reflection of the growing intellectual confidence and competence of Americans, that the first subscription library was founded by Benjamin Franklin in 1731. The library was the outgrowth of the Junto, a debating society (forerunner of adult education and discussion groups) and had fifty subscribers. Other subscription libraries followed: the Redwood Library in Newport, R.I., in 1747, with Ezra Stiles as librarian from 1755–75; the Charleston Library Society, in 1748; and the New York Society Library, in 1754.

The pace began to quicken perceptibly after the 1750s. Political discussion heated up, and the explorers grew bolder and had more thrilling adventures to recount. Franklin's own *Autobiography,* his journalistic reporting, his scientific treatises and urbane essays kept the intellectual community in ferment; Jonathan Carver, a New Englander, wrote a travel book about his exploration of the Great Lakes region and the Upper Mississippi. *The Rights of the Colonies Examined,* by the governor of Rhode Island, Stephen Hopkins, and Thomas Jefferson's *A Summary View of the Rights of British America;* John Adams' vigorous responses to the passage of the Stamp Act in the Boston *Gazette*—later issued as a book; and above all, Thomas Paine's *Common Sense* and *The American Crisis,* provided the rationale for the Revolution, and brought the Colonies to the brink of war.

By 1775 there were some thirty-seven newspapers in the Colonies. Of these twenty-three were classed as Patriot, seven as Loyalist, and seven neutral, or of doubtful loyalty. Their average weekly circulation rose from around 600 in 1765 to as much as 3,500 in 1775, a tribute to the interest and involvement created by events.

Library development boomed in the climate of new opportunity and responsibility that followed the Revolu-

tionary War. The subscription libraries, the "society libraries," the lyceum libraries, and the mechanics' libraries (for
the benefit of the young workingman), began to spring up
even before most states had achieved statehood, to feed the
lively discussions from which pioneer Americans hammered out their new nation. Farmers and workingmen,
housewives and children, began the process of democratiz-
ing learning in earnest. Noah Webster produced *The
American Spelling Book*—widely known as The Blue
Backed Speller—in 1783, and over the next hundred years
it sold an estimated 70 million copies! Alexander Hamilton, James Madison and John Jay wrote *The Federalist*,
and the great debate over centralized versus decentralized
government had begun. Several states established state universities in the immediate post-war years, among them
North Carolina, Virginia, Georgia, and Vermont.

Ohio was the frontier, the first state carved out of the
huge territory created by the Northwest Ordinance, passed
by Congress in 1787. According to its terms, ". . . knowledge being necessary to good government and the happiness of mankind, schools and the means of education shall
forever be encouraged." Even before statehood, the private
library of Revolutionary War hero Israel Putnam was
brought to Ohio Territory by his son and shared, by subscription, with neighbors as the Belpre Farmers Library, in
1796. A town meeting of transplanted New Englanders in
Ames Township, near Athens—settlers who had brought
their love of books with them, but not their books—led to
the formation of the Western Library Association, better
known to history as "The Coonskin Library" because each
of the subscribers contributed from five to ten pelts to get
it started. The coonskins were sold in Boston to purchase
fifty-one titles, and the library was established in 1804.

The first society library to be incorporated by a special
law of the Ohio legislature was in Dayton in 1805, with an
annual membership fee of three dollars. Between that date
and 1817 there were some twenty libraries incorporated in
the state of Ohio, with seventeen others in the planning
stages. The passage of special laws for each one incorpo-

rated had by this time become so burdensome that the state legislature passed a general law providing for the incorporation of school and library "companies."

In that same year, 1817, the governor of Ohio, Thomas Worthington, requested the use of contingency funds to start a state library. Undoubtedly, he was inspired by the organization of the Library of Congress, which had been established in 1800, with the private library of Thomas Jefferson as a nucleus. Nonetheless, the governor himself chose the titles—509 of them—in a Philadelphia bookstore on a trip back East. Along with "how to do it" titles on such subjects as sheepraising, the governor selected volumes of general literature, "to bring within the reach of the representatives of the people such information as will aid them in the discharge of important duties they are delegated to perform."

Thus, Jefferson's *Notes, Malthus on Population*, Clarkson's *History of Slavery, Paradise Lost*, and Gibbon's *Rome* were present to enlarge the vision of officers of the state of Ohio and members of its general assembly. Pennsylvania, New York, Illinois, and New Hampshire were among other states to develop state libraries, and by 1840 some twenty-two states had organized them for the intellectual enhancement and on-the-job education of their legislators.

U. S. Government statistics on education reveal that from 1775 to 1800 some twenty public/community libraries were formed; some 179 between 1800 and 1825; 551 between 1825 and 1850; and 2240 from 1850 to 1875. Apparently, it was an idea that spread pretty fast once it got started, and more and more people kept developing the need to know. In 1802, thirty-four shares at ten dollars each were sold to start the first subscription library in Cincinnati; in 1803 the town of Salisbury, Connecticut, contributed officially to support of a children's library founded by a Boston publisher; and in 1833, the town of Peterborough, New Hampshire, set aside a portion of the state bank tax to purchase books for a town "social" library which was mainly supported by membership fees.

Exploration, settlement on the frontier, trade, and Indians engrossed the country during the early 1800s. The most famous of all authors of the period was James Fenimore Cooper, who virtually invented the American historical romance, and played heavily on the theme of the clash between "primitive" and "civilized" values on the frontier. Henry Wadsworth Longfellow was poet laureate of an era marked by nostalgia, sentimentality, and not wanting to think too much.

The feeling of "let down" in the country as a whole was reflected in the uphill battle for financial support faced by the various types of public library forerunners. Financial panic and political uncertainty in the "mother cities" of the East did not help, and tax-supported schools were beginning to compete for funds and citizen interest. Americans were pioneers again, on the move West, busy with survival; in the machismo atmosphere thus created, reading and libraries in some degree faded from interest for a while. But not altogether.

The rise of concern for setting limitations to the workday and for gaining access to education was directly reflected in the establishment, beginning in the 1840s, of apprentice or mechanics' libraries geared to the need of the young working-class man to learn new skills that would ensure him a role in emerging industry. The Young Men's Literary Association, established in Cleveland became, with generous assistance from the Case family and cooperation from professional societies, an outstanding research and reference library and was later incorporated into what is now the library of Case-Western Reserve University.

At the other end of the "needs" spectrum—and the social scale—were the libraries that grew out of the "lyceum era." The National American Lyceum, pioneer effort in adult education, was organized in New York in 1831, and by 1834 there were town lyceums in fifteen states. Lyceums were formed as associations for the purpose of hearing lectures and holding discussions. In many cases, libraries were begun as part of this activity, which was intellectual and cultural, as well as philosophical, in nature. The climate of the lyceum discussions was greatly influenced by Transcendentalism, the loosely knit philosophical vision of which Ralph Waldo Emerson was the principal seer and spokesman, and Henry Thoreau the most dramatic exponent.

Transcendentalism focused upon man's mystical unity with nature, and the uniqueness and truth of the individual's own apprehension of experience. It was the expression of revolt by a generation against the triteness, orthodoxy, and blatant materialism of its day, and its rejection of dogma or moral authority other than one's conscience and convictions.

Ralph Waldo Emerson was the platform lion of the lyceum era. In the years before the Civil War he brought culture, and thought, and spiritual elaboration beyond the rough demands of frontier life to hundreds of towns on the "lyceum circuit" of the North and West. His personal appearances and his dynamism created an enormous demand for his books and those of other authors ushered in on the waves of the new openness of thought and inquiry. Among these others were Nathaniel Hawthorne, Herman Melville, Edgar Allan Poe, and Walt Whitman. In the same period, Francis Parkman celebrated the way West, and James Russell Lowell, John Greenleaf Whittier, and Harriet Beecher Stowe joined in roundly attacking slavery. These writers, with the lyceum discussions, greatly heightened the growing sentiment against slavery, and widened the gap between those who hated, and those who espoused it.

Undergirding and facilitating this vigorous American literature, a well-established publishing industry in Philadelphia, New York, and Boston adopted, in 1830, the stereotyping of plates, which made it possible to make cheap reprints of pirated English authors such as Scott and the socially conscious Dickens.

Major reforms in the development of schools were set in motion by Horace Mann, secretary of the Massachusetts

State Board of Education, and Henry Barnard, secretary of the Connecticut Board of School Commissioners, in 1838–39. Free school acts were hammered out and passed in various states during the 1840s and 1850s, among them Connecticut, Pennsylvania, New York, Rhode Island, and Michigan. The 1852 Compulsory School Attendance Law was not passed by all states, however, until 1918.

There was a close and symbiotic relationship with library development. The passage of the School Act in Ohio in 1853 provided tax support for public schools and for forty-four libraries established in Ohio school districts, where some of the former subscription-library book collections became the nucleus of the new school libraries.

In 1851, the state of Massachusetts enacted a law which permitted towns to tax inhabitants for the support of free libraries, and in 1852, the city of Boston appropriated five thousand dollars for public-library development. The great waves of Irish, German, and Scandinavian immigrants who landed in New York and Boston, and some of whom fanned out into the farm areas of the Midwest, spurred awareness of the need for education. By 1876, there was a state library in each of the states which then existed, and there were an estimated 188 tax-supported public libraries in the United States, out of an estimated 2,200 or so.

The organization of the American Library Association during the nation's Centennial Year, in Philadelphia, did a great deal to galvanize the forces for growth; 103 persons, of whom 13 were women and one third of whom were public librarians, attended the meeting. Melvil Dewey, who originated the first practical system of book classification (the Dewey Decimal System) was the forceful and imaginative leader who wrote in the first issue of the *Library Journal* in that first year of ALA's founding: "there was a time when libraries were only open at intervals, and visitors came occasionally, as they would to a deserted castle or a haunted house. Now many of our libraries are as accessible as our post offices . . ."

For millions of Americans this was, at the time, "aspirational" thinking in the extreme, but Mr. Dewey did his best to push the vision toward reality. Librarian at Columbia College, it was he who founded the first library school —the New York State Library School, in 1887—to provide basic training in the technical skills of librarianship.

Some big-city libraries (Cleveland for one) developed their own programs of in-service staff development for personnel on the job in libraries, but Melvil Dewey's six months' program taught a uniform sequence of classification and cataloging skills, as important steps to better user access. Librarianship, struggling to find a professional hallmark, somewhat confused the means with the end, and for the next half century defined itself overmuch in terms of technical skills and processes. Indeed, as late as 1939 it was possible for Henry Seidel Canby, professor and bookman, and presumably better acquainted with librarians than most, to write that, "training as a librarian means being a specialist in the techniques of book getting, and book keeping." It was also in this last quarter of the nineteenth century that librarianship and library use both began to appear to be largely the province of women—an image which is only now, and slowly, being overcome. This was a direct result of a social milieu in which the men were lustily devoted to making money, and had little time to devote to educational or cultural matters in general, or to libraries in particular.

In the small-town libraries, the librarian most people saw and knew best was (typically) a gentlewoman with a better-than-average education who shared her interests with others who came to seek. These librarians learned the job by doing it, as did most lawyers, doctors, and other professionals before the advent of special professional training. Yet these librarians provided a ladder upon which literally thousands of poor, or limited-background youngsters climbed out of the underclass and into leadership.

On the user side, the women's club movement turned to the development of libraries as a means of making life more interesting in the small, dusty towns of the Middle West, the plains states, and the Far West. Success was money, and money could be made—and usually was—by the unlettered and the uncultured. The literature of the period was tough and virile, and authors like Bret Harte and Mark Twain celebrated the American virtues of brawn over brain.

There was another author, more widely admired perhaps than many a better one who embodied the values of the period: Horatio Alger. Oddly enough, it was a kind of Horatio Alger type who opened the door to stabilized public support for libraries: Andrew Carnegie, who immigrated to the United States from Scotland with his poverty-stricken parents when he was thirteen years old. Working his way up from "bobbin boy" in a factory and telegrapher in a Pittsburgh telegraph office, he never forgot the books from the private collection of some four hundred volumes which helped him to achieve the status of industrialist and philanthropist. It was in 1881 that Carnegie made his original offer to donate buildings for public libraries to any municipalities which would adequately finance such a library with annual tax appropriations to develop and maintain a book collection and services. In this way local tax support was levered from communities who grabbed at the "carrot" of a free building. At the time of Carnegie's death in 1919, more than twenty-five hundred library building gifts from Carnegie dotted the land, with many more to follow under the terms of his will.

The start of professionalism, the new interest, the buildings, came just in time to enable American libraries to meet their finest hour thus far. The greatest challenge came in the cities, into which flooded the second great migration of working-class people into America—this time from Italy, Austria, and Russia. Hundreds of thousands of them were Jewish, filled with reverence for the Word, the Book, and Learning, and eager to become, as quickly as possible, "real Americans." For many of the others, too, libraries were havens of civility and individual attention in teeming neighborhoods. Some library-centered adult education classes equaled or surpassed those being undertaken today.

Services to children, pioneered by a handful of talented, dedicated women librarians were among the great new looks in library services in the early part of the twentieth century. This activity paralleled concern for child welfare and child labor laws. Public library children's departments were founded in New Haven, Brooklyn, Pittsburgh, Cincinnati, Omaha, Denver, and San Francisco. Prolific and wonderful authors of the late 1800s who had written a rich literature for children included Frances Hodgson Burnett, Louisa May Alcott, Mary Mapes Dodge, Joel Chandler Harris, Margaret Sidney, and of course, Mark Twain. Kate Douglas Wiggin, Howard Pyle, and dozens of others were current and prolific also, and several children's story magazines—paramount among them the incomparable *St. Nicholas*—kept good material coming month by month. A Children's Library League was begun in 1897 by Linda Eastman, then deputy director of the Cleveland Public Library (and later herself the director); over 14,000 children were enrolled, and a special children's room opened in 1898.

Awareness of library responsibility for meeting the needs of special user groups started at about this same time with the beginning, in 1897, of public library service to blind readers through the Library of Congress. When the library moved from the Capitol to its new building, a room was ready, with 550 Braille books, daily readings, and weekly musical recitals, when the library opened. Herbert Putnam, Librarian of Congress for forty years, began national interlibrary loan to the blind in 1900.

Traveling library departments out of state libraries, and big-city libraries, were initiated in several states before 1900, and deposit stations were set up in Grange halls, small neighborhood stores, fire stations, and women's clubs. Their purpose was to "furnish good literature; strengthen small libraries; and to create interest in the establishment of new libraries." Collections of books could be kept in homes, factories, and clubs, too, for varying lengths of time, often several months.

A position for a library organizer was authorized by law in Ohio in 1898, and an "organizer" for extension services established in the job in 1906. The first traveling library in 1898 had been a horse-drawn book wagon, and county-wide service sprang up in several states at about the same time, among them Maryland, Indiana, Ohio, and New York. Demonstrations of countywide and regional services occurred from the early 1920s on.

In 1925, the Carnegie Corporation—continuing the commitment to libraries by the most grateful reader of all time—made a grant to the state of Louisiana, through the American Library Association. The grant was for $50,000 to be spent over a three-year period. When Essae Mae Culver drew up a library demonstration plan, there were only five public libraries, and a handful of college and school libraries, in the state. Miss Culver had to open an office in Baton Rouge, establish a reference service for legislators, and get enabling library laws on the books, while at the same time starting her first demonstration in Richland Parish! The state had never appropriated any money for libraries, but soon after the demonstration in Richland began, the tax commission appropriated $5,000 for maintenance.

The development and demonstration methods evolved in the '20s in Louisiana were so sound and so well conceived that they remained a reliable guide for experiments with larger-than-local units of service in Georgia, North Carolina, Tennessee, Missouri, Arkansas, and other states—many of whom, with neither the advantages nor the disadvantages of well-established small-town libraries—could "start from scratch" on a wider canvas.

The Great Depression created a major crisis for libraries of all types. But public libraries—whose funding was perhaps the most precarious—proved again to be sensitive social barometers, responding to practical needs with survival information and providing, in many a city and town, a place to go where there was light and heat, and for many, spiritual sustenance and escape from trouble. In many places, good use was made of WPA projects to develop library programs, collections, and buildings, union catalog projects, collections of maps and guides.

One unfortunate legacy of the depression years which libraries have had a hard time shaking off, is a psychology of poverty, of lack—and a habit of undue care for petty expenditures, and also for the use of trained librarians to do less than professional-level work.

Still, in some areas, progress slowly continued. Expansion of rural service was made possible in Ohio when the first state aid bill in 1935 provided $100,000 for the 1935–36 biennium to reinforce for extension work all tax-supported libraries. This was raised to $150,000 the following biennium. By 1940, almost every one of the eighty-eight counties in Ohio had county-wide service, and in 1939, the permanence of the state-aid grant was almost insured when it was made a part of the regular budget of the State Library.

National leadership played an important part—that of ALA and many of its leaders individually. In 1938, libraries and their basic role in education were accorded some measure of recognition with establishment of a Library Services Division in the Federal Office of Education. In 1939, a remarkable man began five years of service to librarianship and to his country as Librarian of Congress. Archibald MacLeish took over, on the threshold of world war, and despite the protests of ALA and library leaders because he was not a professional librarian, what had been essentially a one-man fief for forty years. It was probably, in retrospect, an extraordinary instance of the times and the occasion calling to the right man.

Here was a poet, and a fearless believer in freedom of the mind, who saw libraries and librarianship clearly *as they could be*. Throughout his tenure, he shared his vision, not only with the Congress and the intellectual community at large, but with the library profession. Perhaps as much as any single person, he helped to awaken a new sense of dignity, greater and wider self-expectations, in librarians themselves, and nudge libraries up the road from "reactive" to "proactive."

"Libraries must be active, and not passive agents of the democratic process," he said. "Libraries," he told the world, "are the only institutions in the U.S. capable of dealing with the contemporary crisis in American life in terms and under conditions which give promise of success.

"Libraries owe an affirmative obligation to the people. The people have a right to such service, to someone to interpret between the books and those who need them—as much right to know from public servants what books are pertinent to their problems of self government, as to know from public servants what jellies they should conserve, what seed they should plant, and what hen mash will produce eggs."

Mr. MacLeish had some things to say about librarianship, as well:

"Librarianship is one of those activities which can be a job, a profession, or an art, depending upon how it is practiced. If it is a job, you get paid. If it is a profession, you give it your life . . .

"The Librarian in our time . . . is the counsel for the situation. His client is the inherited culture entrusted to his care. He—more than any other man—must represent this client as its advocate. Against those who would destroy the tradition, he must bring the force of the tradition. Against those who would destroy the monuments, he must bring the beauty of the monuments. Against those who would limit the freedom of the inquiring mind, he must bring the marvels of the mind's discoveries."

And Mr. MacLeish spoke, too, across the years to librarians—and thanks be, their number is diminishing—who persist in thinking of their work in terms of processes and print alone, rather than in terms of mixing users with *all* media:

"The physical book is never more than an ingenious and often beautiful cipher by which the intellectual book is communicated from one mind to another, and the intellectual book is always a structure in the imagination.

"If it is the physical book of which the librarian is keeper, then the character of his profession is obvious enough. He is a custodian, as all keepers of physical objects are custodians, and his obligations are a custodian's obligations. He is a sort of check boy in the parcel room of culture. His duty is to receive the priceless packages confided to him by the past, and to redeliver them to the future against the proper stub . . . He must be reliable, orderly, industrious, and clever. He must devise infallible and complicated ticket systems to find the parcels on the shelves. He must read the notations of origin and ownership in a dozen tongues. He must guard the wrappers from the risks of time and theft and matches and men's thumbs. He must be courteous and patient with the claimants. And for the rest, he has no duty but to wait. If no one comes, if no one questions, he can wait.

"But if it is not the physical book but the intellectual book of which the librarian is keeper, then his profession is a profession of a very different kind. It is not the profession of the custodian, for the intellectual book is not a ticketed parcel which can be preserved by keeping it from mice and mildew on a shelf. The intellectual book is an imagined object in the mind which can be preserved only by preserving the mind's perception of its presence. Neither is the librarian's profession the profession of the check boy who receives and guards and redelivers to the future—for the intellectual book is not a deposit of the past which the future has a right to call and claim. The intellectual book is a construction of the spirit, and the constructions of the spirit exist in one time only—in that continuing and endless present which is NOW. If it is the intellectual books of which the librarian is keeper, then the profession . . . must become . . . the affirmative and advocating profession of the attorney for a cause . . ."

The service of libraries during World War II was imaginative, innovative, and diverse: to industry on the home front, to the troops overseas, to children and families left stranded in unfamiliar places, and in need of information and recreation. The public library in Detroit, for example, had a vital wartime Information Center—precursor of the Information and Referral Center program for which it is famous today. A Library Information Section was a part of the Office of War Information. Through it, and other war-related services, government officials learned about librarians and libraries and their "crisis competencies" while, on the other hand, librarians learned about bureaucracy and politics, and how to work with federal officials, and publishers, who were also actively involved in OWI and its programs.

And so, because they had grown with America, had been part of its development from the beginning, and had responded to—and often helped to stimulate—the people's need to know, American libraries were as well prepared as any agency—and better than most—to face the challenge of the post-war years.

Chapter III: New Life for Libraries—the 1950s and '60s

At about mid-century—1950—a whole new world began for America and for American libraries.

Homes were re-established, new families were under way; men reclaimed their jobs in the plants or went to school. It was time to settle down to the pursuit of happiness. Library leadership sensed that the time had come to make some big moves—some giant steps toward the development of library services that would require some degree of financial responsibility for libraries at the federal level.

The storehouse image had begun to fade. As early as 1949, there were thirteen regional libraries in Georgia, and others, supported by state and local taxes in North Carolina, Arkansas and Missouri; regional libraries in Illinois and Washington were supported by local taxes alone. California had developed some excellent county libraries. Still, as one observer put it, "Apart from the enthusiasts, there was no demand for public libraries. The public did not ask for them. They did not know that they needed or would use them. They did not, on the whole, even know that books had anything worthwhile to give them. It was only when there *were* public libraries that most people had any realization that they had anything to give. In other words, here is a case where supply created demand, not where demand created supply."

If this were true, there seemed to be little chance that demand would increase while 88,000,000 out of 131,669,275 (1940 census figures) had either no library service at all, or very inadequate services. Of the 3,068 counties, hundreds—about one county in five—had no library services of any kind.

Some groundwork was laid before World War II had even ended, and immediately after. Ralph Dunbar, director of the Federal Office of Education Library Services Division; Ralph Shaw, then librarian of the Department of Agriculture; and Paul Howard, chairman of the Federal Relations Committee of ALA, met to plan a strategy in 1944. One important outcome was the opening of an ALA Washington Office in October 1945, with Paul Howard as director.

The decision was made to approach the needs of the many millions of people who had no library service, or grossly inadequate services, by beginning with those living in rural areas. Since these were people who, by and large, had no access to library service of any kind, initial programs would show most striking results. Also, the composition of the Congress seemed likely to guarantee the most interest and support for extension of library services in rural areas. Years of developing some library service where there had been none, especially in the South, had laid some good groundwork and provided some patterns.

It was agreed that the legislative program would be developed through the ALA, but with the active assistance and involvement of other organizations, especially component programs of the Department of Agriculture, with its extension network that reached all members of the rural family (Home Demonstration, 4H, etc.).

Paul Howard did the first draft of the Library Demonstration Bill—later to evolve as the Library Services Bill—for the Republican Policy Committee in 1945. The organization of library trustees, which had formed under the ALA umbrella in 1890, was committed to active support, as were other organizations.

The first bill proposing support for general public library services and programs was first introduced in both houses of Congress by Emily Taft Douglas of Illinois and Lister Hill of Alabama (House and Senate respectively) on March 12, 1946, in the Seventy-ninth Congress. On

February 28, 1948, it was introduced again, and passed, this time by the Senate, with George D. Aiken of Vermont joining with Lister Hill in sponsorship; it was introduced in the House, and lost. Again in 1949, the Bill was reintroduced in the Senate, with Hill and Aiken joined this time around by Paul Douglas (husband of the original House sponsor) and in the House, where it was defeated, after a five-hour debate, by a vote of 161 to 164.

By 1949, Bernard Berelson, then dean of the Graduate Library School of the University of Chicago, had completed his study of *The Library's Public: A Report of the Public Library Inquiry*, and had concluded that, "the major correlates of reading and library use are the education of the reader and the availability of reading resources." Another study found that more than half of the adults of the nation lived within a mile of a public library, yet only about a fifth of them had visited one during the year previous to the survey. On the other hand, sociologist Dr. Robert D. Leigh found in his study of *The Public Library in the United States* that nearly 50,000,000 people who lived outside of the cities—in towns, villages, and unincorporated areas—were without access to public libraries. It appeared that public libraries, at least, were serving only from 15 per cent to 25 per cent of the population.

Post-war studies and standards for school libraries indicated that fewer than half of the nation's secondary schools had libraries worthy of the name, and there were virtually no libraries or library programs in elementary schools. Some elementary schools—or more likely individual teachers—borrowed "classroom collections" on long term loan from the inadequate stocks of the public library —some of which maintained "school departments" to try to deliver books on a more or less regular basis. Most schools were rigidly textbook oriented, and few teachers felt the need for supplemental or alternative materials.

Some other significant events were taking place with a bearing on the forward march of library development in general, and the gathering of support for federal legislation in particular. In 1946, the publishers, fresh from their good experience in wartime co-operation in the distribution of the paperback Armed Forces Editions, and through the OWI's Office of Books in Wartime, reorganized a general trade book association under the name the American Book Publishers Council. Its predecessor associations had been dissolved in the 1930s. By 1949, a few statesmen among the publishers had realized that the low estate of reading, and of education in general, would need to be reversed if a nation of book readers (and book buyers) was to develop in the post-war world. They saw it as their social responsibility, as well as being in their business interests, to help effect this. At about this same time, a study of access to books and reading matter was undertaken is a single state with large rural areas—it happened to be Ohio—which showed that many thousands of alert, relatively well-educated people in the farm belt of this otherwise well-endowed state had little or no access to books or libraries. The study, known as The Ohio Project, pointed the publishers in some of the same directions already sighted by the library leadership.

To provide an instrument for action, the Publishers Council formed The Committee on Reading Development, and set it up as a partially separate entity. A bright, energetic, and idealistic young man named Theodore Waller, fresh from service in government and international affairs, was enlisted to run the CRD in 1950. He began picking up and weaving together the threads of initiative spun off by the librarians, the interest of the Department of Agriculture, and other groups. A seminal conference on Research in Reading was held in January 1951. Library Inquirer Bernard Berelson chaired the conference, which involved, in addition to other library leaders, Dr. Robert D. Leigh (already deeply involved with libraries through his study); Dr. Morris Janowitz and David Riesman; opinion researcher George Gallup; the Yale Law School's Harold D. Lasswell; and several leading publishers.

The Committee on Reading Development, in co-operation with the American Library Association, was instrumental in initiating and planning the next move in the development strategy: The Conference on Rural Reading, convened by the Extension Service of the U. S. Department of Agriculture on September 24–26 of that same year—1951. The CRD and the USDA Extension Services Division were joined in this endeavor by the American Association of University Presses, the American Booksellers Association, The Adult Education Association of the United States, and the National Council of Teachers of English. The Sears Foundation provided some funds, and the prepared papers, proceedings, and recommendations were published in paperback format on a not-for-profit basis by The New American Library, as *The Wonderful World of Books*.

Some 130 extension workers, representatives of the organizations involved, authors, librarians, and staff members of universities and government agencies discussed the information needs and lack of library access of rural people. Library of Congress Assistant Director Verner Clapp and Deputy Director Dan Lacy were significantly involved, as of course were Dr. Ralph Shaw, Paul Howard, and David H. Clift, formerly of the Yale University Library staff who had that year become Executive Director of the American Library Association.

The Library Services Bill, meanwhile, continued to gain support in the House. Julia D. Bennett was in charge of ALA's Washington Office when it was again introduced to the floor in 1951—this time with identical bills by eight representatives. In the 1953 introduction (Eighty-third Congress) six more senators joined the pioneer three, including John Sherman Cooper of Kentucky, Frank Carlson of Kansas, Mike Mansfield of Montana, Henry M. Jackson of Washington, Irving Ives of New York, and William Langer of North Dakota. In the House, thirteen identical bills were introduced.

In 1953 perhaps the wave of anti-intellectualism was at its peak; interest in ideas, in freedom to read and think probably reached its cyclical low for the century. In May, the strengthening coalition of librarians and publishers laid another important cornerstone. With almost perfect timing it developed and bugled across the nation the Freedom to Read Declaration, a statement of principles which the New York *Times* praised subsequently as "a great state document." Issued by the ALA and the American Book Publishers Council, it was drafted in large part by Dan Lacy, Deputy Librarian of Congress, who had in that year become the executive director of the American Book Publishers Council. Many other associations concerned with the life of the mind and freedom of the intellect thronged to the banner and asked to endorse the statement that librarians and publishers had made, and the cause of reading and library development made many new and articulate friends.

Many of these new friends joined the CRD and the ALA in founding the National Book Committee in 1954. Formation of the National Book Committee was a response to the realization that librarians and publishers alone could not satisfactorily stem the tide that seemed to be running against the life of the mind. A catalyst was needed to rally all the forces—groups and individuals—which could be counted upon to support intellectual freedom, and the right of all Americans to have convenient access to books and other library resources.

Among those who felt moved to constructive action were a television network executive, a labor leader-statesman, the president of a large manufacturing company, the editor of a Sunday newspaper supplement, a prominent Wall Street lawyer, and the head of the world's largest advertising agency. They joined a number of authors, educators, librarians, and publishing leaders—all people of vision and commitment, to spearhead the effort. Together they enlisted a group of book lovers, believers in the social mission of books, who welcomed the opportunity to give voice to and represent the broad constituency for reading and libraries that exists beyond the ranks of those professionally involved with them.

This "Society of citizens, devoted to the use of books," was spurred into action by intellectual-freedom issues, but its membership of gifted questioners of the status quo was determined to examine and define all the component parts of the committee's stated purpose: "to keep books free, make them widely available, and encourage people to use them." The Book Committee pledged itself to "concern with the social and cultural implications of books . . . the strengthening of library services . . . the fostering of conditions in which diverse ideas and manners of expression can find both publication and readers . . . drawing public attention to matters of public policy which may be involved . . ."

Why, committee members wanted to know, could people in an open society be so swayed by demagogues? Why were the schools not doing the job they should be doing in teaching reading and in developing the habit of reading? Why were homes not motivating children to read, to wonder and to inquire? Why couldn't TV be used to stimulate the desire to read, to the mutual enhancement of books and the audio-visual media? Why were libraries so little used, and so inadequately supported?

The National Book Committee was committed to the encouragement of creative writing; the recognition of literary excellence; the development of reading motivation through every possible channel; creation of public awareness of the value of reading; better access to books and other materials; improvement of the image of libraries and librarians; and above all, involvement in striving toward these objectives of citizens from a wide spectrum of professions, organizations, and economic and social classes. ALA joined in giving life to this "third force" because it believed that librarians and library associations could not alone develop the relationships with other fields, tap the resources of creative help from the art and business worlds, involve a wide range of laymen, and provide a multi-faceted viewpoint of problems and possible solutions needed to mount a library and reading awareness program, or muster political clout needed to broaden use and support patterns.

Thus, when librarians and trustees went confidently back to Congress with the Library Services Bill in 1955, they went with a host of new backers and new political strength. This time the bill went to the floor with thirteen Senate sponsors, with five more asking to be added to the list; in the House, twenty-seven identical bills were introduced by representatives from eighteen different states. But it was June 19, 1956, before the bill became Public Law #597, and was signed by President Eisenhower.

The new law authorized $7,500,000 to be spent for public library services to people in rural areas—areas defined as those with a population of 10,000 or fewer people. Federal funds were to be matched by the states on the basis of per capita income in the state compared with average national per capita income. Each state was required to submit a plan for approval by the library section of USOE— which became the Library Services Branch. Administration of the program was the responsibility of John G. Lorenz, who came to the national job from being assistant state librarian in Michigan.

Unfortunately, the first appropriation voted in July of 1956 was for only $2,050,000—less than a third of the authorized amount. Of this, $40,000 was allotted to each state, as a base.

The states to which this small but welcome windfall came varied widely as to existing library development. Massachusetts and Rhode Island were providing some kind of library access to all their people. Almost all Massachusetts communities, for instance, had libraries of some kind, but more than half were operated on budgets of less than $6,000 a year, and were open less than twenty hours a week. Georgia and North Carolina estimated that they provided for some 95 per cent of their citizens in some manner, and New York, Pennsylvania, Ohio, and Michigan for 90 per cent.

At the other end of the scale were such states as Mississippi and West Virginia. Accessibility, estimated in population density and geographic terms, did not take into account the exclusion of Black people from most public libraries (still legal at that time in the southern states) and access was still thought of in terms of physical nearness. Consideration was of those who thought they wanted to go to the library badly enough to get there, rather than in terms of psychological readiness, motivation, or any degree of real convenience.

Arizona and Utah began their first state library agencies in order to be able to receive and administer the federal funds. Most of the other state agencies turned from being quiet bureaucratic backwaters of state government into better-staffed, more professional and wide-awake agencies with money to spend for program, and a job to do. In the West and Southwest where few libraries had been established, there were single counties—counties larger than some entire eastern states—where no library service existed. In New Mexico, three adjacent counties formed a region more than twice the size of Massachusetts. For an area of some 17,684 square miles, the population averaged about one person per square mile; such a light population, widely scattered, had made it impossible to provide any kind of library service before the advent of federal funds.

Each state agency had to decide where to start. Some believed that a better demonstration could be made by providing library service where there had never been any before; others elected to build on existing strengths, and extend fairly good service to nearby areas. Some states served the chosen localities directly, by establishing state operated branches or centers, or through bookmobile service; others provided existing regional or county libraries with the wherewithal to extend service to their outlying areas. The thirty-seven state plans approved by March of 1957 showed major needs to be: professional personnel, automotive equipment, books and materials, surveys of what already existed, and in-service staff training and development.

By 1958, thirty-three states had made provision for county libraries in their plans. The state by state situation varied widely. Arkansas, for instance, had passed legislation to permit counties to levy their own taxes for library support in 1948, while Oklahoma did not pass such a state legal provision until 1960. By the time the Library Services

Act was passed in 1956, Louisiana, an important forerunner of LSA-type demonstration, had forty-five parish (county) libraries in operation, independent and tax supported. Seven more were added by 1960 with the leverage to produce matching funds of LSA. Methods developed in Louisiana greatly helped other states and regions.

In January 1960, when extension bills for LSA were introduced into the Congress there were fifty-five sponsors in the Senate (a record number) while fifty-two individual bills—also an astonishing number—were introduced into the House. This was vivid testimony to the overwhelmingly good reception of the federal library program, and the need for its continuation. The extension had the support of President Kennedy's administration, something the original bill had not.

One very convincing factor for thrifty-minded congressmen and senators was that a comparatively small amount of federal money had stimulated and produced a sizable increase in state and local funding effort. Thus, for the fiscal year 1960, the funds actually budgeted by fifty states were divided as follows, for support of public library programs: federal—$7,098,185; state—$9,053,139; and local—$4,181,028. The federal money had stimulated nearly twice its own amount in state and local effort.

As a financial transfusion was being infused into community libraries, the librarians, the publishers and the citizens' committee they had together helped to bring to life, realized that the meaning of "library" must undergo a complete transformation if widespread use was going to occur. In August of 1955, a Gallup poll had revealed (George Gallup was a member of the National Book Committee) that 61 per cent of American adults could not remember having read any book—except the Bible, in some cases—during the previous year. It appeared that none of the agencies in the complex reading motivation equation was doing what must be done to create readers and library users: not the homes, or the schools, or the communications media. The public was not in touch with the professionals responsible for planning to meet their intellectual needs or their everyday informational needs. The professionals involved in reading and libraries had little voice in policy making or in funding decisions. People were hesitant to adopt the prevailing "egghead" image of reader and library user as their own; parents were uncertain and too acquiescent before the admonition of the schools not to teach their children to read at home; and schools too often destroyed reading enjoyment by concentrating too relentlessly on skills.

Clearly, the public had little understanding of what good libraries were, or what they could be. Public expectations needed to be raised. The era in which it could be assumed that the obligation to provide library service was fulfilled by simply maintaining collections of books for those who wished to seek them—at whatever effort or inconvenience might be necessary—had come to an end. It seemed evident that the interrelated problems demanded a frontal attack.

First it would be necessary to get the attention of a vast, indifferent public, shake up apathy, and create awareness that would open up avenues for tackling the situation on various fronts. A subcommittee of the Book Committee, chaired by author-historian Marchette Chute, proposed the program that was to become National Library Week. Planning began in 1956. Before authorizing the campaign, the Book Committee surveyed community leaders, librarians, newspaper and book editors; the survey indicated, "overwhelming interest in, and potential for" the umbrella awareness-information-promotion program that was to become NLW.

Gilbert W. Chapman, then President of Yale and Towne, and first chairman of the National Book Committee, announced plans in April of 1957; the ALA announced its participation at the Kansas City Conference of July 1957. NLW was sponsored by the National Book Committee in co-operation with the American Library Association, and the week of March 16–22, 1958, was to be the first week.

Marchette Chute summarized the original aims:

"Its purpose is to encourage the people of the U.S. to do more reading . . . The first emphasis of Library Week will be on libraries, to make our fortunate citizens realize the value of the vast free treasure that is spread out over the land, and to help them learn how to use it at full capacity . . . It will focus also on the vital importance of the school library, the college library, the home library."

It was agreed that all media should be involved—radio, television, magazines, newspapers. From the start, the Book Committee refused to allow the NLW program to denigrate TV or any other medium in its efforts on behalf of reading and libraries. Its theme was always reinforcement and co-ordination, not competition. Just as the Committee sought to expand the meaning of "library," so it worked also to expand the meanings of "reading" and "literacy." As part of its program, the National Book Committee worked, largely but not exclusively, through NLW to establish the concept of "visual literacy" and to help the public to learn to reject the narrow vision of one medium replacing another. It sought the integrated use of books with all other carriers and instruments of communication, to provide a full range of alternatives in style, depth, format and language, as well as substance.

The message of NLW overall to the individual, was that the purposeful library user has an increased capacity to positively affect his destiny, and that of his community, his country, and his world; that training in the library laboratory could enable him to enter confidently into the world of communications—print and non-print—as a transmitter, as well as a receiver; that libraries could help him to develop a positive self-image in terms of his own cultural heritage, and an empathetic understanding of others; and that libraries could provide awareness of opinions, options, and choices.

At a different level, the NLW message to community leadership—political, social, economic—was that libraries of high quality are essential to a democratic society in all its facets; that only careful study of the needs and resources of each community could assure the extent and

quality of materials and programs needed; and that libraries were too important to be left solely to librarians—citizens from all walks of life needed to take a part in making them responsive to diverse needs for information,
education and recreation, and self-realization.

Several events of widely differing orders of magnitude
occurred just before, or during the early years of NLW,
which gave it added impetus and depth, and helped it to
demonstrate that libraries were an idea whose time had
come. The first of these was the publication, in 1955, of a
book called *Why Johnny Can't Read*, by Rudolf Flesch,
which sent ripples through classrooms and PTAs throughout the country, and began what Dr. Jeanne Chall was
later to call, "The Great Debate about learning to read"—
the methods, the reasons why it mattered. Another, even
more significant, was the School Desegregation Act of 1954,
which focused public attention not only on the poor quality of education available to Black children, but to many
others as well.

Then, during the fall of 1957, as state plans went into
effect under LSA, and the professional staff for NLW organized the first observance, the Russians launched Sputnik, an unparalleled scientific achievement. U.S. politicians, parents, and the general public turned in full force
to blame the inadequacy of the schools which had failed to
prepare American scientists to be first into space. The
NLW theme and poster, showing the earth surrounded by
menacing clouds, and exhorting, "Wake Up and Read"
(prepared and announced before the Sputnik launch, in-
cidentally), did press the point home, and gave added impact to the first promotion effort for reading and libraries
nationwide.

It was in response to Sputnik that the first piece of federal funding for public elementary and secondary education, with implications for school libraries, came along in
the National Defense Education Act of 1958. Some of this
money could be used for books and other instructional materials in the specified areas of science, mathematics, and
modern foreign languages. Since libraries were not

specifically mentioned in the regulations, it was a hard fight by school librarians—state by state, school district by school district, and often building by building, to get any of the money allocated for school library resources. Enough people were successful to give a spark of new vigor to library programs in the schools, and some new dependence upon them by teachers seeking materials.

It seems obvious, in retrospect, that a good sense of timing and care in orchestrating library support initiatives with social, educational, and political realities, has paid off. This has been especially true in the case of school library-media centers and programs, and development of support for them.

In 1958, when NDEA Title III provided money "for books, other than textbooks, and other materials and equipment," for instruction in the three subject areas, NDEA co-ordinators at the state and district level refused, at first, to channel any of the funds into purchases for the school library. The majority of elementary schools had no libraries anyway, and those in the junior high schools and high schools were, by and large, inadequate. Reluctance to allow school librarians to buy materials with NDEA funds, or even to integrate materials purchased by math, science, and language teachers with library materials, stemmed in large part from basic ignorance by administrators (and even some librarians themselves) of the fundamentally instructional role of the school's library program. School libraries were considered to be "enrichment" resources, and occasionally, service centers for teachers.

Subsequently, schools found that they had a messy time of it trying to organize and sustain effective use of materials and equipment purchased by various teachers, departments, and classrooms. Equally messy, and frequently embarrassing, were the mistakes made by eager and inexperienced purchasers when confronted by hordes of salesmen with new and glamorous "hardware"—the ubiquitous and largely unused "language labs" were a prime case in point. Thus, by the time the new ALA *Standards for School Library Programs* came out in 1960, administrators were ready to study them, and begin to accept the logical and enormously helpful vision of school library program potential which they spelled out.

For the next five years everything possible was done to disseminate, dramatize, and achieve understanding and implementation of those standards. The Book Committee and Library Week staff worked in concert with leadership of the American Association of School Librarians on almost every phase of implementation. The Standards were introduced to the press, and a comprehensive program of fact sheets and articles resulted, acquainting the education community and the public with what children were missing if they did not have good school libraries.

A state-by-state school library development project, funded by a grant from the Council on Library Resources (an arm of the Ford Foundation set up to manage library grants) and involving school librarians and other educators with political influentials and state-wide organization leaders, was most successfully carried out. In February 1961, an invitation conference of leading educators met to discuss the role of books and other materials in the schools, and expressed the strong conviction that libraries and their resources must become primary tools of learning and teaching, and regarded as a requirement for every elementary school. Thousands of copies of the conference report, edited by James Cass of *Saturday Review*, were distributed.

Early in 1962, responding to an interest sparked by an NLW article on school library lacks (and fanned by William I. Nichols, a major Sunday supplement editor, and a founding member of the National Book Committee), the Book Committee staff assisted the American Association of School Librarians in applying for a grant of $1,130,000 from the Knapp Foundation. The money was to provide for demonstration, in eight schools in different parts of the country, of good school library-media programs. The project's film, . . . *And Something More,* brought to life the role of the library in the school, and the range of printed and AV materials it could make available, for everyday use by children and teachers.

The Knapp School Library Demonstration Project, which ran from 1963–68, provided for visitors to go and see for themselves; it sparked state-oriented demonstration programs in a number of states. Its findings and the recommendations of its advisory board were issued as occasional papers throughout the life of the project; they helped to change, and heighten, professional expectations of school libraries, as the demonstrations and their attendant publicity helped to raise public expectations. A further grant of more than a million and a half dollars to ALA for the study of the training of school library manpower, was also the result of this collaboration, and the success of the original program, which was expertly directed throughout its five years by Dr. Peggy Sullivan.

A series of annual national awards, conceptualized by the Book Committee-school librarian collaborators, was initiated under the sponsorship of the Encyclopaedia Britannica, in 1962. These awards provided publicity reinforcement to the other school library activities. They highlighted the importance of good resources for all the children in the schools of a district, counteracting the tendency to establish a "one-school showcase" type of improvement. They underlined also the vital role of citizen involvement, responsibility, and action in the provision of school libraries.

Finally, in the cluster of primarily public-oriented programs was the campaign carried out on behalf of the Book Committee and AASL by the International Paper Company. Kits on "How to Get the School Library Your Child Needs" were mailed to hundreds of thousands of PTA and other parent and community leaders at just the moment for maximum impact. The need for school libraries had been established, and the time for action was at hand. In several states, the packet of step-by-step how-to-do-it material was sent to every school system with the blessing of the Chief State School Officer; in Utah and Florida, among other states, it helped to achieve passage of a state aid allocation earmarked especially for school library use.

Public interest was strong. An article by Francis E. Keppel, the U. S. Commissioner of Education, placed in *McCall's* magazine in connection with the NLW program, confirmed that concern had reached national proportions. The article called for major improvements of school libraries, which it labeled "a national disgrace" in their inadequacy. It was Mr. Keppel, who, as Commissioner of Education, had responsibility for developing education proposals for the administration to present to the Congress, and the landmark education legislation proposed by President Johnson's administration in January of 1965 contained a special title—Title II—for the provision of school library resources and instructional materials.

The Elementary and Secondary Act of 1965 authorized $100 million to be spent by the states for school library resources. Allocations were based on the number of children enrolled in public and private schools within the state in relation to the number enrolled in all of the states and the District of Columbia. Funds were also allotted to the Department of Defense, and to the Bureau of Indian Affairs, for their special school systems. Chief state school officers were required to develop a state plan, and materials were to be made available on the basis of relative need by children and teachers. Library resources were defined as books—including textbooks—periodicals, documents, audio-visual materials, and related library materials. To insure that the legislation would furnish increased opportunity for learning, Title II materials were not to supplant, but supplement, those already being provided.

Only in the first year—fiscal 1966 (July 1, 1965–June 30, 1966) did the actual appropriation come up to what had been authorized, although subsequent amendments increased the funding authority from $100 million the first year, to $220 million by fiscal year 1973.

Meanwhile, between 1960 and 1965, public library development had gained fantastic momentum. The "consciousness-raising" effected on the public by the combination of exposure and demonstration, citizen involvement and publicity, had helped to reinterpret the role of libraries in the light of present-day needs, and helped enormously to raise public expectations (and professional expectations as well) of what public libraries should be able to do for people. The climate of library awareness was working to the benefit of all libraries—including college and even special libraries in businesses and institutions.

It had become apparent that the federal role in assisting the development of public libraries must be expanded beyond the rural confines of the original LSA. A major factor was the growing evidence of the end results of the population explosion, and wartime shifts of rural, often undereducated, people to the central cities, coupled with the exodus to the suburbs of (mostly White) middle-class families in the '50s. These population factors were combined with the shrinking opportunities for unskilled and undereducated city dwellers as technology-oriented industry—which in any case had little place for them—followed skilled, middle-class workers to the suburbs.

In May 1963, the National Book Committee gathered together a group of urban sociologists, librarians, and city planners at the Harvard-MIT Center for Urban Studies, to consider the problems of the new immigrants to the cities, and the financial and service problems their needs would present to public libraries. The report of the Symposium on Library Functions in the Changing Metropolis was published by the MIT Press as *The Public Library and the City*, edited by Dr. Ralph Conant. This conference, funded by the Council on Library Resources and the Joint Center for Urban Studies of MIT and Harvard, helped to set the stage for attention to the growing plight of urban libraries as their local tax base disappeared, while their potential clients required—though many of them did not realize it—greater services than most libraries were able to provide for them.

In 1964, then, the Library Services Act was enlarged to become the Library Services and Construction Act. Construction grants, provided by Title II of the expanded act, were first available in fiscal year 1965, and proved over the next few years to give great impetus to use of and interest in, libraries. Librarians had noted that new or remodeled buildings increased use dramatically; now, for the first time, libraries could get out of old, forbidding, and inconvenient buildings and into inviting, street-level facilities. By the end of fiscal year 1972, more than 1,800 public library buildings had been built or remodeled to serve some 60 million Americans. About $159 million in federal funds had been matched, as of that date, for this purpose, by $399 million in state and local funds—a ratio of $1.00 in federal monies to $2.50 in state and local funds.

Participation in LSCA required each state to have a plan approved by the Library Services staff of the U. S. Commissioner of Education. It provided funds for books and other materials, equipment, salaries and other operating expenses, for state-wide planning and evaluation of programs, and for administration of the state plan. Emphasis was on strengthening metropolitan public libraries, and so enabling them to better serve as regional backup resource centers, and to develop and improve services to persons without service, or with inadequate services. Subsequent authorization cycles, regulations, and priorities assigned to LSCA during the period 1964–71 provided a Title III to promote interlibrary co-operation; improvement of library services to the physically handicapped, the institutionalized, and disadvantaged persons. Funding authority was increased substantially with each new authorization.

Passage in 1964 of major legislation aimed at ameliorating the lot of the poor and minorities was to have tremendous future implications for the development of all—but especially public—library programs. The Economic Opportunity Act of 1964 focused attention on early childhood learning, the importance of preschool development of a positive self-image, and concept development as a base for later successful learning in school. Public library children's librarians had been eying school library development with some apprehension, and groping to reshape their roles as bookmobile visitations and classroom collections to schools became unnecessary. Emphasis on preschool children and their mothers—especially in the city ghettos—caught their imagination and professional vision, and many began to plan and carry out programs in connection with Head Start—one of the most popular and viable of the Office of Economic Opportunity's programs.

In 1966, at the request of the Bureau of Libraries of USOE, the National Book Committee contracted with the Office of Economic Opportunity to survey and analyze library-related services to the disadvantaged at the neighborhood level, and to make recommendations for libraries who wanted to engage in outreach services. The report, called *Neighborhood Library Centers and Services* projected the potential of public libraries to render service to the culturally isolated, racial minorities, and the poor in both cities and rural areas. It emphasized especially the need for libraries to engage in information and referral services, and act as a community switching station for help to users. The report described experimental programs in libraries in ten states, and recommended the establishment of model, multi-purpose, multi-media, neighborhood centers with strong library components.

More than 15,000 copies of this report were distributed to public libraries and community agencies, and it was influential in helping to give direction to subsequent library outreach programs. In that same year, Bernice Mac-Donald's survey of *Literacy Activities in Public Libraries* focused attention on the library's potential for serving the functionally illiterate adult. Spurred by the new LSCA responsibilities, the OEO programs and the implications for literacy of the Civil Rights Act of 1964, the Adult Services Division of ALA, the Book Committee and the American Book Publishers Council had been pondering the problem of too few low-reading-level/high-interest-level materials available. A conference in April 1964 brought together educators, labor leaders, manpower experts, librarians, and publishers to explore both needs and markets for material suitable for adults with minimal literacy.

By 1967, when the National Book Committee, under contract to the VISTA component of OEO—often called the Domestic Peace Corps—devised kits of paperback books for use in VISTA Centers and community agencies, there were a number of useful books to include for functionally illiterate adults. With an advisory committee of librarians, and funds supplied by the Ford Foundation, books for children, young adults, and adults, and reference books, were chosen especially for use in migrant camps, on Indian reservations, in urban and rural slums, and in mental hospitals. The project enlisted the help of state library agencies in developing ongoing relationships with VISTA workers and their clients, the great majority of whom had never had any experience with libraries. VISTA programs were eventually to have their effect on public libraries, once officials and VISTA workers began to understand that reading and libraries were relevant to providing opportunities for the poor.

It was not until 1965 that a third major type of library, serving an ever-growing segment of the population—the college library—was provided with its own earmarked library title. The Higher Education Act of 1965 was the first to specifically designate assistance for college libraries, although it is true that colleges were the first educational institutions to receive federal aid, beginning with the Morrill Act and continuing with subsequent vocational education provisions. The plight of the colleges without any such aid as that granted to the land-grant colleges was probably dramatized by the explosive development of the community colleges, which had to start from scratch, in the early sixties, to provide higher-education opportunities for the huge post-war generation. Unlike the established private universities, these institutions had no rich alumni, and no money to provide for libraries. Theirs was only one case of extreme hardship, for all the institutions of higher education were hit hard during the sixties and after, even the major state-supported universities.

Title II of HEA was designed to improve college libraries, and the quality of library services by providing funds for the purchase of books, periodicals, and other library materials. It included also a part that authorized training programs for librarians, and research in and demonstration of new ways of programming, processing, storing, and distributing information. Title II also authorized funds for the Library of Congress to acquire and catalog additional scholarly materials.

Part A of Title II HEA provided for grants, on a matching basis, to institutions of higher education, their branches, or to combinations of institutions. The grants could be used for books, periodicals, documents, magnetic tapes, phono-discs, AV materials, and other related library materials, including law library resources. Three types of grants were specified: basic grants, supplemental grants, and special-purpose grants. Basic grants were to be made before any of the other two kinds were made. All grants were to be approved by the U. S. Office of Education.

Basic grants were for $5,000 to each institution, to be matched on a dollar-for-dollar basis. Previous levels of expenditure were to be maintained, and new institutions were permitted to apply for basic grants in the fiscal year before students were actually enrolled. Supplemental grants, to be awarded after all requests for basic grants had been satisfied, were to be made to the extent of $20 per student (or equivalent) to institutions which demonstrated special need. Special-purpose grants were meant to meet special institutional, regional, or national needs of either a single college or a combination of colleges. Matching funds of $1.00 for every $3.00 of federal money was required and the maintenance of effort included.

Part B of Title II provided for grants to institutions or agencies for training, and covered short-term or full-session institutes, establishment of fellowships, or traineeships with stipends. Another section of Part B provided, to institutions of higher education or other non-profit agencies, money for innovation and programs improvement, for which proposals must be submitted and reviewed.

Part C of Title II authorized the Commissioner of Education to transfer funds to the Librarian of Congress for the purpose of acquiring, insofar as possible, all library materials currently published throughout the world which are of value to scholarship; providing and distributing catalog and bibliographic information promptly, and enabling exchange of materials not readily obtainable outside the country of origin on behalf of institutions of higher education and non-profit research libraries. Part C made possible the development of the Library of Congress MARC (Machine Readable Cataloging) System which will increasingly make possible time and money savings in the processing of books and other media.

Details of the tremendous new financial commitments to libraries that came about in 1964 and 1965 would not be complete without mention of the Medical Library Assistance Act of 1965 which provided $13,800,000 to the National Library of Medicine to develop the medical library network. Here is a special library system whose life-and-death responsibilities held obvious personal interest for every member of Congress and for all citizens. MEDLARS (Medical Literature Analysis and Retrieval System) enables the medical professions to gain speedy access to citations—over 2 million of them—from journal articles from 1964 onward. With its federal funds, the National Library of Medicine can also sponsor experiments in communicating medical assistance to remote regions. Terminals for MEDLINE (MEDLARS on Line) are in use in some 250 medical libraries in the United States and Canada—in medical schools, large hospitals, and VA and Defense installations.

By 1966 then, the role of the federal government in the support of libraries of all types had been well established, and justified in any number of ways, such as the greater freedom of teachers to personalize instruction, and the far greater numbers of users. Since the advent of LSA and support for public libraries in 1956, the accelerated momentum of events had made increasing demands upon libraries, and it was clear that library services were needed —if not yet fully accessible—to a greater or less extent by the entire citizenry: rich and poor, Black and White, highly educated or undereducated. Exposure and experience with libraries had touched millions of potential new clients, and a realization, overwhelming in its implications for both society and the library profession, had begun to emerge: libraries in the future would need to be prepared to meet the needs of Americans along a spectrum ranging from the illiterate, isolated, and handicapped to those in the vanguard of intellectual, scientific, and technological achievement.

In September 1966, President Lyndon B. Johnson established by Executive Order, a National Advisory Commission on Libraries which was to report back to him in terms of the following questions:

What part can libraries play in the development of our communications and information exchange networks?

Are our federal efforts to assist libraries intelligently administered, or are they too fragmented among separate programs and agencies?

Are we getting the most benefit from the taxpayer's dollar spent? The National Advisory Commission on Libraries was to aid the President's Committee on Libraries (made up of administration officials, including the Secretary of Health, Education and Welfare, the Librarian of Congress, and others) to:

a) make a comprehensive study and appraisal of the role of libraries as sources for scholarly pursuits, as centers for the dissemination of knowledge, and as components of the evolving national information system;

b) appraise the policies, programs, and practices of public agencies, and private institutions and organizations, together with other factors, which have a bearing on the role and effective utilization of libraries;

c) appraise library funding, including federal support of libraries, to determine how funds available for the construction and support of libraries and library services can be more effectively and efficiently utilized; and,

d) develop recommendations for action by government

or private institutions and organizations designed to ensure an effective and efficient library system for the nation.

By the summer of 1968, when the commission submitted its report to the President's Committee of administration officials, American life had been convulsed, its youth embittered, its economy endangered, by the Vietnam war. The war brought incalculable change to American life, already shaken by the "discovery" of the poor, and the bitterness and revolt of the Blacks and other racial minorities. Out of the protests, the marches, the murder of political leaders grew—in the words of *Newsweek,* "the counter culture, and a whole new politics that changed the role of women in society and gave a new voice to every other alienated sector of the society." President Johnson, the President who had come closest to making library access to all people a matter of administration policy, was driven from office by the burden and the hatreds of Vietnam, and the foundation era for library support and development had come to an end.

Chapter IV: What Libraries Do for People

Despite social, political, and economic pressures, librarians have continued to reshape and expand librarianship into a diverse and dynamic profession. Some areas of work have been developed to a high degree, and a variety of activities carried out superbly well, in a wide range of settings.

A new feeling of power and responsibility pervaded the profession as it learned to reach for and utilize funding from sources other than those marked, "for libraries." Librarians left far behind the age-old stance of being ready to serve those who found their way to libraries; passed quickly through the stage of wanting to take library materials and programs out to people who would not come in, but wanted them. By the time they reached the end of the '60s, most librarians were ready to assume the more sophisticated and difficult responsibility of *motivating* use— of stimulating the desire, and the sense of need for information in those who had not developed it.

In public libraries, there was vastly improved information and reference service, and in many cases referral service, to users at both ends of the complexity spectrum: researchers, businessmen, art lovers and students, on the one hand, and people seeking survival information about health, food, and housing on the other. Special projects were developed to implement such national priority programs as Right to Read, career and vocational education, drug-abuse prevention, early childhood education, and opportunities for the aging, the handicapped, and minority citizens.

By the early 1970s, state library agencies in most states had become effective arms of state government, and had begun to look at their responsibility for state-wide library development in terms of all types of libraries, not public only.

By 1974, some 130 library co-operative projects, involving some 10,500 separate libraries of all types, had been set up under Title III of the Library Services and Construction Act, so that delivery of library services and the use of library resources could be made more effective. Many of these projects involved planning of a cross-type-of-library (involving school, college, research, and public) within the states, while others were of a multi-state regional order.

In the late '60s and early 1970s, librarians found that groups of potential users were articulating their needs as never before and that such needs could not always be met with traditional patterns of service. Beginning in July 1971, each state was required to develop a comprehensive five-year plan incorporating state priorities, procedures, and activities in terms of user needs. Annual program plans outlining projects to be undertaken under each LSCA title also have to be submitted. Most of the long-range plans include attention to co-ordinating the resources of public, school, college, research, special, and other libraries within each state, and in some cases, across state lines.

There are now, for example, eighteen library systems in Illinois. Each system serves a population of some 150,000 persons or more, and each has two or more public libraries co-operating to give the best possible service to every citizen within the service area. Only the Chicago Public Library, one of the eighteen, is in itself a system with the three-level responsibility of providing local residents with service, functioning as a research and reference center, and undertaking the interlibrary responsibilities of a system.

There are 538 public libraries included in the Illinois

systems—with only 11 left to go. Within the past two years, state regulations have redefined "systems" to include academic, school, and special, as well as public libraries, so that a true total network of service is in progress. Five of the suburban library systems surrounding Chicago serve 3,000,000 people through 168 libraries. What exactly do they do for them?

Well, for one thing, fast delivery can move material from one library to another within forty-eight hours. Within the North Suburban system alone, half a million people have reciprocal borrowing privilege, and can find out through the union catalog what each of the other member libraries of the system has that they might want. Two of the large surburban systems have pooled their audio-visual services, and share a large film collection. They also provide a high-speed duplication system for filmstrips and other AV materials. One system has initiated a books-by-mail service, and sends a tabloid-style catalog by mail to homes in outlying areas.

Another kind of system is developing within the city of Chicago itself. The Chicago Public Library has begun to build regional service centers within the city which will serve as "back-ups" to the branch libraries and residents of an area. The first regional center, or spin-off subsystem, will serve more than 100,000 people on the South Side— heavily Black—section of the city. In it will be housed an outstanding Afro-American History and Culture collection —the Vivian Harsh Collection; a fully equipped auditorium suitable for every kind of sight and sound presentation; an atrium-type garden area with sculpture in it; study facilities with carrels equipped for the use of AV equipment and materials of all kinds; two lounge areas, for browsing, dreaming or just thinking.

The Woodson Regional Center is close to five high schools and at least four post-secondary institutions. It will be a *student* center primarily—but not geared only to young students. It will have a visiting scholars' room with lockers for research material and desks with typewriters; and there will be two conference rooms, with tables for seminars and meetings. There will be a large area for microforms and periodicals, and the audio-visual area will not only contain a tremendous collection of AV materials and equipment for loan and use, but facilities for production and reproduction of materials and media.

Library of Congress classification will be used throughout the collection. The section on the Social Sciences is planned for some 67,000 books; the section on the Humanities and Fine Arts for some 60,000 titles; the Science and Technology section for 32,000. Color coding will be used to direct clients to various service areas, and large, colorful graphics, using Library of Congress classification and subject headings, will be used throughout the building. There will be reference desks for ease in using reference titles, and books will be housed on low shelves for greater accessibility. Periodical indexes for each subject area will be close to the areas to which they pertain. There will be an abundance of microform readers, reader-printers, and coin-operated copy machines.

The Woodson Regional Multi-media Center is in many ways the library wave of the future. Since the early sixties, media centers have developed primarily in schools, community colleges, and other educational settings, but Woodson forecasts what many public libraries will be in the future. The staff that will be assigned to the subject areas is being trained specially to interrelate print with non-print materials; to encourage the production of materials by the branches in the Woodson region; to develop programs jointly with the community—and the communities that surround the branches in the region; to play a distributive role for phonodiscs and cassettes for clients; and to provide entertainment and recreation as well as information and educational services. The center has set up neighborhood citizen groups to advise it on all matters of physical layout, staffing, materials, and program.

Like many other public libraries, the Chicago system is becoming more and more involved in providing opportunities for continuing adult education. Its program called Study Unlimited is jointly sponsored by the City Colleges of Chicago. The program got under way in 1973; there are five study centers operating now, and more planned. Many people with less than a high school education begin with Basic Literacy and other basic education subjects and move on into preparation for the GED, or High School Equivalency exams. Counselors from the college work with all students; those in the GED program are referred to the County Superintendent of Schools, who makes arrangements for them to take the examination and receive their diplomas when they are ready. Many of these students, having gotten into the swing of self-directed study, keep on going and into the College Level Examination Program (CLEP), in which they may receive a total of twenty-four semester hours of credit for college courses by taking examinations as they are ready for them.

Some eight hundred adult learners are at present involved formally in Study Unlimited. The student's classroom is his local library branch. Each student proceeds at his own pace, his study hours set to suit his own convenience. Materials used include Sony video cassettes, texts, and related readings. The curriculum is the core of courses which are essential to general education and lead to the Associate in Arts degree. Review cassettes are available for those who want to prepare to take credit by examination. The counselor from the college system meets with the student at the library, and the TV teacher may be contacted by phone or in person, and meets periodically with the student in the library.

The City College System and the Public Library System share responsibility for providing the structure for a high school or college level program of study for the student. In this case, it is the college which provides accredited instructional opportunity in new and flexible formats; establishes administrative procedures that fit both the needs of the independent learner and the requirements for academic standards for an accredited college; provides adequate guidance and counseling in academic and career decisions; and allocates credit due for non-instructional and life experiences as well as for formal instruction completed.

The Chicago Public Library, as the other partner in the enterprise—or one of the other partners, if the student is to be considered a partner, as he should be—develops the library into a good learning environment by providing adequate study space, and learning materials, print and non-print; reviews, and regularly updates and refreshes, the variety of materials; co-operates with the college system in designing and offering group events which reinforce individual learning, such as workshops, films and exhibits; and most important of all, establishes the "learning advisory services" which provide students with highly personalized assistance in finding and using materials effectively. Librarians may be called upon to teach sessions on library use, basic reference, simple research techniques, the use of the book or card catalog, and the resources of the library. Strong commitment to people, and to helping them to achieve their own goals, is required of librarians and other library staff members who can successfully guide people in the use of resources which they may never have used before.

Texts and study guides for independent learners are available at each of the Chicago Study Unlimited Centers. Each student is assigned two viewing hours a week at the video player at the time most convenient to him. If he is able to come at that time he is assured the use of the equipment; if he cannot make it for some reason, no one gets upset. Each course is composed of from fifteen to thirty taped lessons, and the video tapes can be edited, labeled, and stored as easily as books. One study console with TV monitor will provide some ten to twelve viewing periods per day. Audio cassettes are used, too, as are 35 mm filmstrips with sound, but video cassettes seem to be most successful because they are easy to operate, and because of the interest they stimulate by multi-sensory impression.

Examinations are scheduled on an individual basis, since there is no reason for independent study to be locked in to the rigidities of a regular school calendar. Working with learners on a one-to-one basis, helping them to locate and use material, and evaluating their learning success, takes an enormous amount of time and patience, but it is a necessary commitment as the adult independent learner becomes increasingly a central focus for today's public library.

By way of illustrating a variety of patterns in this area, the Sioux City, Iowa, Public Library System carries on a variety of formal and informal adult learning programs geared specifically to Indian people, and in partnership with the Winnebago Tribal Library, the Winnebago Community College at Norfolk, Nebraska, the Indian Council Center, and the Indian Center of Sioux City. Two Winnebago aides, paid by the Sioux City Library (under a special grant from the LSCA), work out of the Winnebago Tribal Library, and furnish material for adult programs run by the community college.

The Indian Library Project at Sioux City has seen as its function getting education projects started with its funds and staff, and then turning them over for continuation to Indian organizations and agencies. The GED program of study to prepare for equivalency exams was begun at the library, and is now operated by the Indian Center—which obtained a grant itself for that purpose. Several Indian young people who began in the Library Project as aides were themselves encouraged to finish high school through the library's program, and are now in college as full-time students. The library has been a collaborator in classes in cooking and consumer education with the Indian Center; in self-expression, creative writing, and public speaking with the Indian Council Center. An Indian-planned media van visits rest homes and senior citizen homes on the reservation. All of this work is carried on out of the Central Library by another Indian aide who works with organizations and individuals.

Public libraries of different sizes and in many geographic locations are involved with the National Right to Read program, and a number of them have been funded from the National Reading Improvement Act (which had only $12,000,000 in federal funds for the current fiscal year to fund the entire national program) to conduct programs for the adult community. One such program fans out from the Arkansas River Valley Regional Library in Dardanelle, Arkansas—a rural regional system which services five counties through eleven branches. Tutorial help is made available to anyone over sixteen years of age in almost any location in the five counties. Funds from its community-based Right to Read grant have been used to develop a media collection geared to the development of the adult new reader; recruit and train volunteers and part-time personnel to help in teaching reading on various levels and in various locations; augment with books and other materials programs already in operation in other agencies; and teach people to read on a one-to-one basis.

Another example of the many interesting and innovative programs that illustrates what today's public libraries are capable of doing for people—and many already are—is that of the Mid-Columbia Library System at Kennewick, Washington. Since 1972–73, two tutors have offered tutorial and information materials—many of which they wrote themselves to meet local needs—to clients in migrant camps and in their homes, where they have met with groups of four to ten people weekly. The adults in these communities have observed that the children are more likely to study when they have the reinforcement of seeing their parents learning too.

When a demonstration project proves itself so well that it is continued with local funding after the original grant period is up, all concerned may feel proud. The Free Library of Philadelphia's Reader Development Project, originally funded through an LSCA grant in 1967 was the only demonstration which the city of Philadelphia approved for continuation with local funding. The program is aimed at young adults and adults who read at an eighth-grade level or below. The project also plans programs and activities for adults and young adults who have literacy skills but are allowing them to atrophy with disuse.

Materials are organized by such subjects as family life, jobs, reading, writing, arithmetic, science, the world and its people. The Reader Project maintains an up-to-date file of, and close contact with, over four hundred organizations who work locally with the undereducated. Communication is carried on by means of a newsletter of which a thousand copies are distributed every two or three months. It carries film and book reviews, news of what community organizations are doing in reading, and other news of interest to personnel in agencies that serve the target audience. Examples of these organizations include: Philco-Ford Project TEAM; Nationalities Service Center; Adult Armchair Education (part of OIC); several correctional institutions, halfway houses, etc. Spanish groups help by "dubbing-in" audio elements in Spanish for sound filmstrips. Special projects include film-making for prison groups, scholarship lists and referral, etc.

Reading specialists may be added to library staffs, or simply "loaned" on a part-time basis by co-operating Adult Basic Education programs or other agencies. Indigenous support personnel must be worked into the personnel-classification scheme and trained to communicate professional expertise to turned-off or unreached potential readers. All public service librarians need training in adult counseling and outreach techniques before impact can be made on the masses of people who need reading skills and guidance. Referral by other agencies—community action programs, neighborhood centers, employment, family service and welfare agencies, clinics—and word-of-mouth recommendations by satisfied neighbors, family, or friends, are the prime way of attracting illiterate adults into a program.

Philadelphia, like many other cities such as Brooklyn, Los Angeles, Atlanta, and Corpus Christi—to name but a few—has mobile media vans that take library materials and programs into the city streets. The Freewheeler maintains deposit collections in medical and health clinics, and other locations where poor people spend a great deal of time. Recognized as a giveaway program to a large extent, built-in plans for return of materials to neighborhood branches nevertheless often start people on the library habit.

Information and referral services that not only give people information but help them to take the first "action" steps with it, are seen as another "wave of the future" for public libraries by many library leaders. Users from Appalachia to Detroit have indicated that they need help in finding out how to solve everyday life problems—coping or survival information, as it is called—about employment, how to deal with bureaucracies, landlords, and legal tangles. Some libraries are already processing information by computer and setting up data banks on all human services in their areas. Some have set up three-way conference capabilities to link patrons to services directly, with the librarian as a kind of interpreter, mediator, advocate, or arbiter.

A grant from Title II B of the Higher Education Act through the USOE Office of Libraries and Learning Resources has enabled a consortium of five city libraries to test, over the past three years, alternative patterns for setting up and operating such services, as Neighborhood Information and Referral Centers. Each of the city library systems—in Atlanta, Cleveland, Detroit, Houston, and the borough of Queens (New York City)—has operated differently. In Detroit, the service is called TIP—an acronym for "The Information Place." In addition to the central file of basic agencies, with names and numbers for the entire city, each of the twenty-nine community branches, has had to add its own local information gathered from business, churches, block clubs, and individuals. Community workers from each branch take community walks to groceries, barber shops, police stations, pharmacies, and gas stations to find out what is going on, and keep in touch with it.

Not all libraries do things like that, but the important thing is, we know now that they *can*. And they have had considerable success in "clueing in" more people in how to get along in a very complex society.

The librarian of one small city—Crystal City in Texas—

exemplifies the orientation and attitude that is spreading to other small-town librarians. She established four priorities for the library: recreation and life enjoyment; active dissemination of survival information; total information services for community leaders and developers; recorder and repository of the culture and history of the community. This library has two paid staff members, and over twenty volunteers, all of whom spend more than half their time working with other agencies on the library's behalf.

This country's population of more than 21,000,000 people over sixty-five has attracted and held the professional attention and efforts of many public libraries. This population includes many who are handicapped or immobile; a large proportion are undereducated, and most of the aging, whatever their economic, health, or social condition, were ill-prepared for retirement leisure. Large-print books and magazines, talking books and machines, cassettes and players, activity directories, home delivery, film programs, and other activities are among the services librarians have thus far devised to serve this group. Libraries from Jackson, Mississippi, to Tulsa, Oklahoma, are trying to reach out into the nursing homes, the senior-citizen residences, and other institutions and homes; but it is expensive work in terms of resources.

Some of the aging are of course lifetime readers, listeners to music, and appreciative viewers of art and travel films, but others never had time in their hard-working lives to learn to use libraries or library materials, or develop habits of recreation, so they are difficult to reach and motivate although library resources may be literally at their doors. One branch librarian in the Cleveland system realized that although a senior-citizen facility was just across the street from the library, few of the six hundred inhabitants ever came in. Hundreds of door-to-door calls and friendly chats later, many of the aged, lonely, and listless people had been developed, by several young library aides, into regular listeners, viewers, and readers.

Public libraries are making an increasing effort to serve men, women, and young people who are in correctional institutions, where redirection and retrieval opportunities are great. Newspapers with news of "outside," law books, and career materials are increasingly part of permanent collections in prisons, and basic literacy training and materials to develop learning skills are often brought in regularly. More and more public libraries are working with drug rehabilitation centers and other halfway houses—where people at a personal crossroads need all the help they can get from libraries: new ideas, new interests, new self-confidence, and new skills.

Among the greatest challenges that all types of libraries have faced, and are facing, is the need to retool their concepts of materials selection, programs and services, staffing and administration, to reflect awareness and meet the needs of a multi-cultural, multi-ethnic, multi-linear (or non-linear) society.

Many libraries are now making a sincere, and on the whole increasingly successful, effort, to meet the needs of the ethnic minorities: the Blacks; the Spanish-speaking of several varieties and locations; and the American Indians. To these millions of people—Americans all—almost everything about the White majority's prevailing culture is seen as alien, and often threatening to self, to family, to neighborhood, to language, to race, and to value system. The litany of lack, the scope of the job to be done are all too familiar: the decayed housing, the dead-end jobs, the total absorption in survival from day to day, the disgust with short-term solutions that characterize the poor among these minorities. A recent phenomenon, as the minority middle classes expand, is the suspicion, the rage, and the social ambivalence of young, educated business and professional Black, Spanish-surname, and Indian people. To all of them, libraries as part of the "put down" status quo, the establishment, are part of the problem until they make strenuous, sustained, and successful efforts to become part of the solution.

An increasing number of libraries of all types—public especially, but also school media centers and colleges—

have shown what can be done when the poor and/or slighted are introduced to library services that are persistently tailored to their needs. This is service that reaches out to people where they are—both psychologically and physically; library service that creates an appetite for more, in surroundings that feel comfortable, and with people who add to the feeling of belonging. It takes books and other media that reinforce each other and have immediate meaning, and experiences with communication that bolster one's sense of worth.

Libraries have found that programs geared to the millions of non-library users who are culturally isolated, poor, and alienated are most successful when they are undertaken in collaboration with all manner of other agencies; provide quiet places to study and think—an antidote to crowded, noisy homes and streets—and most important, user control of programs, genuine input into program planning, and participation in the choice of materials is essential.

The challenge now is to use what has been learned from hundreds of innovative programs permanently to redirect the "regular" program of the libraries. It will not be easy, but it will help to make "American" an even prouder designation than it is now—a name that applies equally to people of many heritages and races, joined together in a free association, but not a melting-pot.

Some people may wonder if public libraries are only trying to "do more" for the non-users of libraries—the poor, the handicapped, and others who must be introduced and enticed. This is emphatically not the case. The huge effort of the past ten years especially has been to enlarge the "user-pool" clear across social, educational, and economic lines. This in fact has been one of the great challenges and the great glories of public library performance: they have tried to gear to the needs of a huge new clientele, while continuing to give good services to their traditional clientele: researchers, professionals, and business people; young parents; and the ever more affluent, better-educated middle class. We have dwelt upon efforts to serve some of those among the millions who constitute the 75 to 80 per cent of the population that have never been library users.

The Denver Public Library, for example, like many others of all sizes, has a "welcome" leaflet which spells out the several levels of service, and how to use them. A street map of the city shows the location of the main library and its nineteen branches. Research collections are emphasized: the Conservation Library (believed to have been the first in any U.S. public library); the Western History Department; the Mountaineering Collection; the Ross Barnett Aeronautics Collection; and a rare book room which includes the Douglas Collection of Fine Printing. In addition, the Denver Library System is a regional depository for U. S. Government documents, a depository for the United Nations and U. S. Atomic Energy documents. It has also been designated as official depository for the materials of the Colorado State Board of Architects; The Colorado Scientific Society; the Colorado State Board of Registration for Professional Engineers and Land Surveyors; and the Colorado State Board of Accountancy. This city library system, like a number of others, is headquarters for a system comprising all of the public libraries in an eight-county system in the metropolitan central area of the state.

Also in Denver, great-books discussion programs, sponsored by the library system are scheduled in all areas of the city—some in library branches, and others in churches or community centers, an international house and a retirement village. Great writing by Plato, Kant, Shaw, Goethe, Marx, Joyce, Turgenev, and others attracts readers interested in sharing their reactions and responses.

The Denver Tomato, a publication by and for young adults is sponsored by the Denver Public Library, and gives an airing to opinions, reviews, poetry on a wide range of subjects, in picture and print.

This library's "new comfortable approach to independent learning" is called, simply "On Your Own." Trained staff help self-directed learners to "organize the information and resources on any number of learning projects—for free, without schedules, grades or fees." The library also offers coaching for CLEP—the College Level Examination Program, mentioned earlier—by which up to two years of undergraduate credit can be earned; and GED (General Educational Development) exam for High School Equivalency. The library also offers a credit course in business and engineering skills through Colorado State University, and an enrichment-cultural multi-media program, "Time Alive."

A vast array of business and reference services are available from public libraries of all sizes, now that even many small libraries have "backup" resources from state or big-city research libraries through teletype, Wats Lines (Wide Area Telephone Service) and computer-assisted searches for data. In the state of Connecticut, there is now an "800" phone number for direct reference help from the State Library in Hartford, and a state-wide library card which allows a resident who is registered with any library in the state to obtain materials and information from almost any other. In Stamford, Connecticut, a suburban city of some 105,000 population which has recently become the headquarters home of several major national corporations, the public library uses, at present, more than 3,600 periodicals in telephone and in-person reference work with the public. In February of 1975, there were some 5,000 requests for information, and the number is increasing each month.

The Tulsa City-County Library in Oklahoma personifies the very best efforts of American public libraries to assess and meet the needs—and further to stimulate the information needs of a broad cross-section of citizens. It has loan collections of art objects, prints, and paintings; lunch-hour concerts and book reviews (people come and bring a sandwich); holds seminars in collaboration with local companies on subjects of interest to business people; and offers adult learning programs for credit in collaboration with local universities and colleges, at five local branches, "Your Know-How Place."

One of the first public libraries to ask for and receive grant funds from the National Endowment for the

Humanities, and collaborate with some of its projects, the Tulsa City-County Library has sponsored forums and lecture-discussion series with Humanities Funding for several years. A recent series which attracted wide public attention and attendance was on "Freedom and Responsibility"—a film-discussion series on the themes: Man vs. the State; Conscience vs. Duty; and Individuality vs. the Common Good.

At the other end of the spectrum, Tulsa has recently launched an ambitious information-recreation program for the aging, to supplement and expand its large present program of special services to shut-ins, nursing home residents, the mentally and physically handicapped, and people with learning disabilities. National Endowment for the Humanities funding, rather than money labeled "libraries" will support the launching of the new aging program.

Some small-town and county libraries have shown unusual initiative and flair in expanding into non-print media in public libraries and programming its use so that it involves users in do-it-yourself communications. The Gale Free Library in Holden, Massachusetts, although housed in a veritable old fortress of a building, obtained video equipment through a grant from LSCA Title I funds. In addition to taping library programs, it is used on loan by town departments, community groups, and individuals who can demonstrate their ability to operate it, or complete the course of instruction the library offers. The Natrona County Library in Casper, Wyoming, uses its video equipment to tape community events for later use, and offers video reference service which can transmit material from library resources directly into a user's home or office. It is also one of the few public libraries to have obtained and operated its own CATV channel, with telecasts directly from the library. The Port Washington, New York, Public Library has used videotape equipment to develop the communications skills of users. All of these are indicators of the library's potential role in the production of materials of local and regional interest, its ability to capture on film and tape some of its own unique resources.

Until quite recently, service to adults in many small town libraries took a back seat to service to children. And indeed, services to children through community or public libraries has been raised to the level of art by America's children's librarians in this century. Freed, in large part since the 1960s, by the development of elementary school libraries, from trying to provide book collections to school classrooms, public library programs for children have blossomed in all directions.

In addition to story hours, always a Saturday morning and after-school success, especially in the middle-class neighborhoods, there are dozens of other kinds of activities, and many kinds of things (besides more books) being lent and used in programs. Cameras, microscopes, paint and clay, and even, in several programs geared to preschool children, live pets, can now be found in children's rooms at the public library. A game corner featuring checkers and a variety of word games can be a center of attraction, librarians have found, and teamwork with other agencies that serve children is constantly expanding and marks such endeavors as outdoor mobile theaters and caravans in collaboration with children's theater groups. Improvisation, dramatic play, and mobile units that give children a chance to look at books and hear stories, are increasingly popular. Puppets seem recently to have had a rebirth of popularity, and toy-lending libraries have a great appeal, in middle-class neighborhoods especially.

Public libraries have sponsored radio story readings and story tellings for many years, and television programs after TV came along. Now, in San Francisco and several other cities, two-to-five-year-olds can Dial-A-Story by using a special phone number, twenty-four hours a day, to hear recorded stories and poems that change each week. Other libraries have prepared special kits for loan to deaf children and others with physical or mental handicaps.

Programs that feature giving children books to keep has been stimulated by the spread of RIF—Reading Is Fundamental—now a nation-wide program of giving books to disadvantaged children which began in Washington, D.C., in the '60s. A group of cabinet wives, spearheaded by Mrs. Robert (Margie) McNamara, began a drive (as a Library Week project, in fact) to collect old books and magazines and give them to children who had no books. The elementary schools of Washington at that time had no libraries, and Black ghetto children especially had little access to books. The project evolved quickly, thanks to Mrs. McNamara's energy and several solid foundation grants, into one in which new paperbacks were given, and schools and libraries were tied in to try to insure that children who got a taste of books would get a chance at more. Local companies and organizations co-operated, and as RIF has grown and spread it has made an ever more significant contribution. Many public libraries have organized similar programs and found relatively small amounts of private funds to give books on special occasions—birthdays, or Christmas or other holidays—and perhaps have a continuing "free and swap" bin, where children can take a book without formalities, put another in instead.

Sidewalk story hours, stories in a tent, stories in vans, bilingual story hours, stories on tape, story festivals—all are happening inside and outside the children's rooms of America's public libraries. Crafts and craft shows; things to handle (snakes, sculpture, and you name it); film and filmstrip programs; film-making and photography clubs, camera trips and shows of pictures taken by children; TV program viewing followed by related stories and activities; art, dance, poetry, and writing workshops; chain reading games; reading improvement and one-to-one tutoring; book fairs and sales; career days and programs: all this and much more is going on for little children to teen-agers. There are of course, still school visits to and from the public library, but these are now inclined to be special "fun" occasions rather than sessions on how to use the library, by children who are well-acquainted users of their library-media centers at school.

A most important and developing aspect of children's work in public libraries is the work done with and through other agencies such as day care centers, community centers, and informal neighborhood-home centers. Programs are jointly sponsored in many locations outside the library and more and more with children's as with all public library service, emphasis is on reaching people where they are, rather than trying simply to "lure" them into the library.

There are an increasing number of libraries which feature parent-education efforts and involve families in assisting small children in early learning and in laying the groundwork for later reading, at home. Reaching children by reaching their parents is usually more effective than trying to reach the children alone; children can be involved with the library staff for only short periods, and home carry-over and reinforcement are essential if language skills are to be developed. Many libraries have introduced related mother-child, or even young child–older sibling programs in which both family members are enjoying reading, listening and viewing at the same time. Such programs are especially important for disadvantaged adults because their example of reading or information seeking will encourage their children. The example of adult models is a prime factor in whether or not children will become readers and learners.

Many libraries now rely heavily on trained neighborhood volunteers—often but not always—parents, and usually, but not always, adults—to read to children, tell stories in the language of the home (Spanish, Navajo, and many others) play word and counting games, lead creative sessions with paint, film, audio cassettes and other activities. Young children will follow the lead, the style, of children several years older than themselves, and libraries have successfully tuned in to this natural pattern of the family and the neighborhood.

School libraries have been almost completely transformed by the attention, and the money from Title II of ESEA and NDEA III, and the materials and resources that have been available to them in the past ten years or so. The development of these instructional media centers has transformed the entire instructional program in many schools. Instructional methods and even the curriculum have been made more flexible and responsive to the needs of individual learners by the use of a wide range of books and other printed and audiovisual materials. Children and young people can now learn independently, and at their own pace; teachers can personalize instruction. The multi-sensory approach to learning has motivated, stimulated and reinforced teachers' efforts and made teaching more interesting and more rewarding.

The most remarkable job of radical improvement in libraries has been perhaps in elementary schools, where, in just over a decade, multi-media resource centers have been created where there was little or nothing. Not very long ago, an elementary classroom was lucky to have a few books on shelves at the back of the room, or in a hall closet or corner of the cafeteria. Although learning to read, and learning to use learning tools, was a basic task of the primary grades, no one expected anyone to enjoy it or to have fun reading while he practiced his skills.

Media specialists in the elementary schools have changed much of that. Children now learn from kindergarten up to look and see, and to relate what they see, feel, and hear to reading and all the other language skills, in their school library/media centers. Many new elementary schools have quite literally been built around the library, so that the library-media center is a second "homeroom," and children are in and out of it all day long. There are carrels equipped with outlets for the use of projectors and other viewing and listening devices; areas for one-to-one tutorial work in reading, math, or other subjects; and small conference rooms for special project work with two or three children at a time: all close to the source of materials. Library/media specialists are master teachers, familiar with the entire curriculum, intimately associated with the reading program, and with the capabilities of each child. The constant exposure and day-in day-out intimacy with many forms of expression fuels curiosity and builds learning expectations.

The primary job of the school library media program and the specialists who create it out of materials, space, and interaction with teachers and pupils, is to support every area of study undertaken in the classroom. This includes science, math, art, music, health and hygiene, in addition to the obvious ones like social studies and language arts. The good program does not offer just enrichment or supplemental learning, but alternative paths to learning for each individual child. Thanks in large part to the elementary school library-media program, it is not unusual to find third- and fourth-grade children undertaking research projects, alone or in small groups, using models (of the universe, spacecraft, or the human body for example) charts, maps, film loops. Further, an increasing number of media centers are so equipped that children may make their own slides, acetates for overhead projectors, audio and video tapes and films, and write their own books, and thus produce their own learning materials to share with other members of the class, or even other classes. The school library media program in many schools has become the creativity program, and the library, the creativity center.

Development of secondary school libraries has been extraordinary, too. Librarians have learned to become—in just a few short years—communications experts who work with television production and microfilm as confidently as they work with books and magazines. They must be able to select—and help teachers and students to select—and organize for program use materials in every form and format. The media specialist has become a full-fledged member of the teaching staff, functioning in curriculum development, planning instruction and evaluating learning, and as accountable as any subject teacher.

Students have broken out of rigid scheduling and use patterns, so that the media center in many schools is now an all-day, after-school, and often evening and weekend resource. New high school buildings often place the school library media center on the ground floor with its own outside entrance, so that it may be used when the rest of the building is closed. School media specialists were quick to see their expanded potential role with a generation of audio and visually exposed children with a wide and growing spread of abilities and interests. Video tape and dial access are used, along with film and other media of all types, yet as librarians have moved into the non-print world they have been increasingly conscious of their responsibility to bring the AV-TV oriented children back to the other end of the communications spectrum, to the printed word. They have realized that no medium replaces any other for all purposes.

School library media specialists have provided an enormous amount of inservice education—albeit informal—for teachers, to help them to update their teaching strategies, and to break out of the much criticized "lock-step" that fits the child into what is supposed to be learned, rather than fitting the learning and its pace and style to the child. Media specialists, recruited increasingly from the ranks of teachers, appreciate what all of this can mean to personalized instruction, and a revolution has quietly taken place in education—one that would hardly have been possible without library media centers.

The third of the major types of libraries which are apt to touch an American during his lifetime—the college library—has undergone a great broadening of purpose and program in the '60s and '70s, as access to higher education has been democratized. The setting apart of the undergraduate library from the major graduate and research resources in the large university was one important step toward making libraries more efficient for students to use; the other was the growth of community colleges.

The community college was an evolutionary step in higher education which combined some aspects of the junior college, the vocational and technical school, and the adult-education agency. The returning veteran fixed identification of community colleges as definitely adult—not a mere thirteenth and fourteenth grade of high school, but a part of higher education; 1960–70 was the great decade of the development of the community college, and for community college libraries. In 1960, about 453,617 students enrolled in them for two-year degrees; in 1970 there were 1,484,000 enrolled and working toward degrees. The community college provides vocational and technical training; remedial or post-secondary developmental general education for those who missed out, or dropped out earlier; and the first two years of a four-year, accredited academic college program—a transition phase —for those who may want to go on to a bachelor's degree.

There were some six hundred two-year colleges in 1960, and close to a thousand by the middle of the 1970s. The bulk of the growth was in the number of publicly supported institutions. Because so many of these started from scratch—suddenly in business where there had been only fields on a county road eighteen months or so before— their media centers were able to start from scratch too. They were planned from the start as total media centers is which non-print mingled comfortably with print. Quarters were designed with proper electrical outlets for the use of all media, and for the convenience of the commuting, usually working, student.

Since the Higher Education Act of 1965, Title I, specified 22 per cent to be allocated for public community colleges and technical institutes, library learning centers benefited greatly, as they did also from the Vocational Education Act, Title II, NDEA III, the National Vocational Student Loan Insurance Act, and the GI Bill. Altogether about a third of the materials for these colleges, both printed and AV, were probably purchased with federal funds, which not only greatly enhanced the library, but also the status of the librarian and his role in planning and in curriculum development. Since the opportunity to develop learning media centers was present, reliance on rigid textbook learning and lecturing was not necessary, to the great benefit of students and instruction. The cost of the initial collections of some 20,000 volumes, figured at a cost of some $10 per volume, was $200,000.

Community colleges have served as laboratories for experimenting with new types of service and materials, including auto-instructional labs, video tape and TV instruction, and graphics studios. The community colleges, by offering training for library technicians, have nudged the library profession into recognizing their potential, and developing some criteria for training them.

As more and more post-secondary institutions adopt policies of open admissions, the demand increases for a great range of individualized programs to meet varied student needs. Many colleges and universities now have courses geared to the needs of the slow learner, the gifted, the bilingual, the culturally different-from-the-mainstream, the underachiever, the veteran, the retired person who never before had a chance to go to college. The sluggish job market for college graduates with years of investment and poor outlook for effective use of their education, will probably send more and more young people into the community colleges where they can learn, live at home, work part-time, and gain skills that have immediate market value. None of the career ladder, independent, interdisciplinary programs can be carried out without a wide range of up-to-date, pertinent library media resources.

Finally, there are the special libraries, both publicly and privately supported, the great research libraries and the special library systems that directly or indirectly affect the lives of nearly every American citizen.

These include the university libraries, the research collections of public libraries, the great government libraries—like the Library of Congress—and the library-research-information centers of industrial companies, advertising agencies, art museums, and science and defense installations: all those whose business it is to serve in depth the needs of the specialist engaged in a particular business, profession, or project. These too, like the libraries at the more general end of the information needs spectrum serve more people in more ways than were to be imagined fifty years ago.

Many of the company libraries, like that of Monsanto Chemical Company, for example, are considered to be so vital to the conduct of the company's business that they are open around the clock, seven days a week, with every kind of information imaginable that relates to the work of researchers, engineers, chemists: reports, abstracts, patents, back issues of journals on microforms, indexes, notebooks, and dissertations on microfiche. The special librarian, often a fellow professional with graduate degrees in one or more subject fields in addition to library science, aids with research. The keynote is service, facilitation, for these libraries are maintained to do their share in a profit-or-loss world, and must earn their keep every day.

The National Library of Medicine, already mentioned, sponsors experiments in medical outreach—a satellite communications system in Alaska, for instance, which enables a health aide in a remote village to be in touch with a physician. Still another special library network serves users directly and through 130 co-operating regional and local libraries. This is the Division of Library Service to the Blind and Physically Handicapped, maintained by the Library of Congress, which mails thousands of titles, recorded and printed in Braille, each day to users of all ages. Brailled music enables a harpist to continue her professional life, and Brailled cookbooks help homemakers. There are even talking books for children combined with Brailled illustrations.

Many of these materials are used by those with other disabilities—mental and physical. Co-operating public and state libraries offer group activities, home visitors who help users learn to use special materials and equipment. But there are only under half a million borrowers of reading aids, talking and Braille books, tapes, and other media, although millions of people are estimated to be eligible for specialized services because of physical handicaps alone.

Finally, a word should be said about state library agencies, the official state presence and facilitator for library services in each state government. In addition to keeping and organizing state documents and archives, providing law library service to legislators and library and information service to other agencies of state government, most state library agencies have responsibility for service to state correctional institutions, mental hospitals, and the smooth functioning of Library Service to the Blind and Physically Handicapped. All this is in addition to administering federal grants to public libraries, developing reference and research networks, and library systems networks, and providing backup service to citizens throughout the state. Now and in the future especially, an essential job will be co-ordinating and developing partnerships among school, college, public and special libraries' resources within the state and across state lines. It is the state libraries which must lead, always with one eye on the reluctant, the fearful, and the inadequate, and the other on the politicians.

And so, thanks to an infusion, for the first time, of significant amounts of money, a new level of professionalism, professional expectation and belief, tremendous vision and very hard work, librarians and their allies had, by the early '70s, moved libraries light years toward greater usefulness to people. They had learned, to quote one library educator, that, "it is only after awareness of short-comings takes hold that the process of change is set in motion . . ." They had, indeed, "created a climate of belief that change is possible," and they had brought libraries into a central role in American life by showing what they could do for people.

Chapter V: The Struggle for Resources: 1968–75

If librarians and their citizen and congressional supporters had learned one lesson, especially during the years in which they worked together to bring information access, through libraries, to the front and center of American life, it was that good-quality library service, like anything else, costs money. The time had definitely passed for librarians as well as for doctors and other professionals, when services could be paid for in chickens and produce instead of hard cash! The little old lady librarian in South Jersey who had been discovered in the 1950s buying books with the proceeds of the sale of plants she raised in the library's windows, had retired, along with those whose communities were content with libraries stocked with the proceeds of bake sales and fine money. The school where, in years before the '60s, the principal had bought such books as suited his fancy or sent out a call for an attic cleaning in the community or a PTA donation to furnish his school "library," had been irreversibly altered too. Communities and schools had learned, in just a few short years, to depend heavily on library resources to which they, in turn, made a regular commitment of support.

Then came the great watershed in the twentieth-century life of America—as wrenching, perhaps, as the Civil War had been in its century. Nineteen sixty-eight brought the My Lai massacre—the Tet offensive—and the horror of the Vietnam war brought home, finally, to all the American people. Life at home turned ugly; violence on the streets and on the campuses forced the resignation of President Johnson from consideration of another term in presidential office. Confrontation marked—and marred—the Democratic Convention in Chicago, and at the end of a long, hot summer and fall, Richard Nixon emerged as the new leader of a Republican administration.

From 1969 onward, a dismaying fact became increasingly clear: equalization of educational and economic opportunity, and development of library and information services for people were to be throttled down. Libraries of all types—central to, and the very symbol of, intellectual diversity and an informed electorate, began a struggle to hold on, at the very least, to the ground they had gained. From the outset, recommendations by the Nixon administration featured major cutbacks in budgets, and the phasing out of library program support. In every case, the funding requested would have provided appropriations for school, college, and public libraries far below the amounts authorized by a bipartisan majority in the Congress.

These actions were in fact in direct contravention of the national policy concerning the provision of library and information services to the American people which had been developing over a decade with support from both political parties, both houses of Congress, and by the Executive Branch. This policy was clearly set forth in a provision of Public Law 91-345, The National Commission on Libraries and Information Science Act of 1970, which was signed into law by President Nixon on July 20, 1970. The provision read:

> The Congress hereby affirms that library and information services adequate to meet the needs of the people of the United States are essential to achieve national goals and to utilize most effectively the nation's educational resources; and that the Federal Government will cooperate with state and local governments and public and private agencies in assuming optimum provision of such services.

The law which contains the statement of policy in its preamble established a National Commission on Libraries and Information Science (a prime recommendation of the study by the earlier National Advisory Commission which completed its work and forwarded its recommendations in 1968) to plan and make recommendations for the implementation of this policy. President Nixon did not appoint members to this commission until 1971.

The first battle in the long struggle to "phase out" federal responsibility for library services began in April 1969. President Johnson had submitted a budget for fiscal 1970 (to begin July 1, 1969) for Office of Education programs in the amount of $3,591,300,000, prior to the inauguration of President Nixon on January 20, 1969—a usual and practical procedure. In March, the new Administration revised the budget down to $3,180,300,000, and in so doing cut out completely all funds for several library programs, including Title II of ESEA for school libraries, and Title III of NDEA. They proposed cutting in half funds of Title I of LSCA for public libraries. The proposed reductions and eliminations were responded to by the organization of a coalition group, the Emergency Committee for Full Funding of Education Programs, comprised of education, library, and other interested groups. Charles Lee, retired former staff member of the Senate Education Subcommittee, was executive director. The Full Funding Committee, like the struggle with the Administration, still continues, the word "emergency" long since dropped from its name.

The first victory, and assurance to librarians that Congress appreciated the value of libraries and knew they must have some federal support, came when a vote to restore funds specifically to education and library appropriations was successful over the opposition of the Appropriations Committee and the Administration. This was an historical "first," and an extraordinary accomplishment at a time when the unrecorded teller vote still existed, and no one could tell how a member had voted on amendments unless the House member could be recognized going through the "yea" or "nay" counting line of tellers. As

Robert Frase, for many years head of the Washington office for the book publishing associations, one of the most respected lobbyists of all time, and a chief engineer of these counter strategies tells it:

"The Emergency Committee and its supporting organizations brought in the necessary constituents and other observers to man the House gallery as well as to set up a "whip system" organized floor by floor in the House office buildings, to get the supporters of the amendment over to the floor when it was time to vote. The techniques for such an operation had been developed by the civil rights coalition in earlier years, and the Emergency Committee had the indispensable aid of a veteran of those earlier coalition battles, Kenneth Young of the AFL-CIO."

The Labor-HEW appropriations bill for fiscal 1970 was not passed until January of 1970—halfway through the fiscal year—and then was vetoed by the President. A substitute bill reduced the appropriations but limited to 15 per cent the amount that could be cut from any specific program, and was signed by the President in March 1970. It contained more than $600 million over his proposed figure, and none of the library programs were eliminated.

Immediately, the fight for the fiscal 1971 appropriations began. The over-all budget proposed by the Administration was about the same, but individual programs were still marked for the ax. By July the now separate Office of Education bill, with more in it than had been proposed by the Administration, had been passed and quickly vetoed. The organizations in the Full Funding Committee again assembled in Washington with large contingents of grass-roots lobbyists, and the House and Senate overrode the veto, encouraged by the show of constituent support. It was not until October that the Administration released the funds in the bill on which library (and other education) programs were supposed to have been running since July 1, 1970.

Library appropriations for fiscal 1972 were well over the amounts that had been budgeted by the Administration, which seemed in a sense to have paused to consider, before rejoining the fight again. An important feature of the 1972 LSCA authorization when it came up for renewal that year was the addition of $15 million for a new Title III—Interlibrary Cooperation. Through this title, grants could be made to the states for the planning, establishment, and maintenance of co-operative networks of libraries at the local, regional, or interstate level. Such networks were to "provide for the systematic and effective coordination of the resources of school, public academic and special libraries and information centers for improved supplementary services for the special clientele served by each library or center." Funding for fy (fiscal year) 1972 was $2,640,500, with basic allotments for each state of $40 million, and $10 million for outlying territories.

Legislative delays and vetoes resulted in there being no fiscal year 1973 appropriation for most education and library programs when the Congress adjourned to go home early for the elections in October of 1972. A so-called "Continuing Resolution"—by which Congress permits spending equal to proposed Administration budget figures or the actual appropriations for the previous year (whichever is lower) until an appropriation has been passed—supported library programs after a fashion throughout the entire fiscal year which ended June 30, 1973. By pegging support to the Administration's budget figure, Congress found that they had drastically reduced or zero-funded some programs, so Congress passed a revised Continuing Resolution in mid-year to improve the situation. This bill required the Administration to spend for individual education and library programs at the level of the lowest previously vetoed appropriation bill. The President ignored it, and withheld funds beyond what had been proposed in his own budget request.

The Executive Branch now had an embittered library and education community, with many new allies to face, and in 1973 part of the fight for funding went to the courts. Suits were filed against the federal government to retrieve impounded 1973 funds appropriated to ESEA (school libraries), LSCA (public libraries) and NDEA (equipment and materials for school and community college libraries), by some twenty-five states.

Meanwhile, it was well past the time for the appropriations for fiscal year 1974. The Executive Budget submitted to Congress in January 1973 for the fiscal year that would begin on July 1, 1973 (fiscal year 1974) completely abandoned any pretense of supporting the established national policy which had been fought for and reaffirmed by librarians, and through Congress by the public, since 1969. Act by act, title by title, this budget proposed to eliminate every penny of federal support for libraries—other than those of the federal government itself. Rationalizations for this "zero funding" had a pincerlike, no-win, and distinctly "damned if you do, damned if you don't" tone. Some of the programs that were alleged to have been unsuccessful were therefore to be terminated. But there were others, which were said to have been successful to the degree that they would be able to "go it alone," with reliance solely on state and local funds.

After a variety of legislative skirmishes, delays, and changes in Administration tactics, a bill calling for $747 million over the proposed budget request and restoring significant library appropriations was signed by President Nixon on December 18, 1973. The following day, in response to the suits, and rather than take issue with the highest courts, the Administration released the impounded funds, some $466 million in education and library monies that had been withheld from fiscal 1973 funds. As finally approved by the Congress, the bill appropriating funds for fiscal 1974 allowed the President to cut no more than 5 per cent from any one program or title.

Thus, after seventeen straight months of library program subsistence under the Continuing Resolutions, an orderly and reasonably secure basis for programs that depended on federal funds was re-established. Success had come from co-operation in a worthwhile cause and as Mr. Frase pointed out, from the spirit "of never giving up, or of taking anything for granted."

At the end of the bout with zero funding and impoundment, the Washington *Post* in an editorial headed, New Life for Libraries, heralded the fact that "the attack of the Nixon administration on libraries appears to have been repelled." It summed up the story well:

> The first argument defending zero funding said that, since the Federal share for libraries was approximately 5 to 7 percent, no libraries would close down when Federal funds were withdrawn. This argument, however handy for rationalizing, overlooks that many library projects are demonstrations . . . A second argument for cutting off funds was that libraries would become part of revenue sharing, thus categorical aid was not needed. When the ALA examined the situation, however, it found that of the 2.96 billion dollars that went out between January and June of this year, libraries received only $21.7 million, or less than 1% of the total.

The report of a "concerned citizens' crisis conference" held in June 1973 explained in even more detail the vital role of the federal support for libraries:

> Basic costs of buildings and salaries are met primarily from local, state and institutional funds. But Federal funds have provided the stimulation, and the means for extended services, for new ventures, for coordination of activities, for enriched programs and innovative materials. . . .
>
> Federal funds have brought school libraries into urban slums, and new branches of public libraries into the suburbs. They have created a market that has made it possible to publish and bring to inner-city children books reflecting their experience and responding to their needs. It has been Federal funds that have enabled school libraries

to acquire new instructional materials in all media. Federal funding has made it possible to create and use new kinds of vocational teaching materials for young men and women with limited reading skill. It is Federal funding, too, that has helped to create the libraries of our hundreds of new community colleges and technical institutes.

At the same time, Federal funds have helped to import and catalog foreign publications to strengthen the advanced research collections needed by our universities and scholars. Federal funds have helped to encourage the development of statewide systems linking libraries together in each state. Federal funds are just beginning to provide the basis for a nationally linked library system.

The National interest cannot be allowed to rest on scattered, parochial and unpredictable local actions.

Against the bleak background of 1973 glowed two promising facts which had become evident: that libraries had demonstrated their validity and usefulness so well that representatives and senators of both parties were willing to go on the line for libraries, and to keep their capabilities growing; and that librarians themselves had grown so much in confidence, in management skills, and in political savvy that they were ready and able to fight for what they needed instead of knuckling under.

By the time the struggle for resources at the national level—which still continues—began, the management of all types of libraries, both at the policy-making level and the administrative level had become much more sophisticated. Long-range planning, the setting of objectives, the utilization of manpower, the making of budgets and cost-benefit ratio factors and accountability engaged much of the attention of adminstrators in all types of libraries.

Public library trustees, for instance, had learned much more about how to fulfill their role as advocates of the needs of the people to be served rather than as protectors of the city budget, trying to see how little the library could "get along" on. Younger, more committed, more innovative citizens had become involved with libraries, and were being appointed or elected to boards. Many boards had at least experimented with budget proposals based on user need and program requirements instead of circulation-based formulas which reflected only one aspect of use, and nothing of user or program potential.

Public library administrators had been required, too, by the 1970s, to study weaknesses and strengths in their operations as never before; to design more flexible budget and acquisitions procedures; to rethink some of the uses of time, energy, and money that had been traditional, scrap some of them, and assign some priorities. The power born of money cannot be ignored, and library administrators armed with their federal monies had learned to deal more forcefully, and from a position of strength, with city and county officials. Many were able, for example, to insist on changes in bidding procedures that were not compatible with efficient operation of the library. The development of consortia, the pooling of resources (film collections, consultant services, for instance) and above all centralized processing, had been an enormous help in making resources go further, and in freeing up time for planning, staff, and program development.

School library media specialists had gained in self-confidence and managerial expertise by the time of the threatened federal cuts. Many more of them had come to their library media specialization from teaching than formerly; as fully credentialed master teachers with media specialization they had more authority with faculty and administration than only library-trained professionals had ever had. True, they too often had little or nothing at all to administer in the way of staff, and many school media specialists were still unsure of their budget allocations for the year. But at least, most had eliminated the conviction—still widely held in the early '60s—that their "real work" had to do more with the acquisition and processing of materials (mostly books) than it had to do with planning with teachers or working with students.

By the 1970s school administrators, from building principals to superintendents of schools, had read widely about and heard much talk at professional meetings, of school library media programs and their essentiality to a good instructional program. This enabled them to make more convinced (and convincing) budget representations to school boards about the school library item in the budget. And again, school librarians gained immeasurably in political stature and clout by reason of having their own title in ESEA, and school board members, younger and more educated than formerly, were not immune to being impressed with the national recognition of the importance of school libraries. School librarians made friends of principals, superintendents, and school board members from the time of the 1960 standards onward, and when the time came to go to bat for Title II, they were ready.

Finally, school library media specialists in many more systems had, by the '70s, a co-ordinator, supervisor or consultant as their advocate in the administration building. The number of district-wide school media supervisors rose tremendously during the '60s. And certainly, the experience gained in arrogating to libraries some of the funds and materials that had come into the schools under NDEA III was valuable to school librarians. From 1959 on, classroom and subject teachers had stockpiled materials relating to science, math, foreign languages, reading, social studies, and the rest, and it had taken skill, good timing, and persuasiveness to meld them, whenever possible, into the central materials resource.

College librarians too, had gained from the federal funding experience in their ability to demonstrate the library's role in relation to students from varied backgrounds, and its support in making possible new course offerings for which there were no readily available texts. Federal cutbacks in higher-education funds for college libraries came, for them, as the colleges' shrinking enrollments were eating away also at other sources of funds.

How, one may ask, have library funds been spent, and what savings have been made in expenditures? Take first the most expensive item, personnel.

It is estimated that some 115,000 librarians were employed in the United States by 1970, together with some 120,000 library attendants and assistants—aides and clerks and paraprofessionals and technicians. The number of attendants utilized (support staff of all kinds) was greatest in academic and public libraries. Some 45 per cent of all professional librarians were employed in school library media centers, and only 16 per cent of the non-professional assistants, because school media centers were still, in most places, one-man (or woman) enterprises with little clerical help. Employment of assistants is expected to rise more sharply than that of librarians as non-professional staff members are assigned more responsibility for routine work, as well as specialized work in outreach, with other agencies, etc.

The employment growth rate over the period 1970–85 is expected to be much slower than previously, with much of the new employment to replace retiring staff, rather than to fill new positions. Employment of school media specialists is projected to grow from 52,000 in 1970 to nearly 80,000 by 1985, but much of the growth will not occur until the 1980s, when school enrollments will again turn sharply upward.

This library employment had great significance in terms of how money was spent and what it was spent for, when the present unstable and unsettled economic situation began. Since approximately 80 per cent of all library budgets—all types of libraries—are spent on salaries and other personnel costs, and since library programs rely heavily on the interaction of people with materials, it is important to note how, and in what degree, libraries have in recent years tried to get more program for their program money by better utilization of professional staff for management, supervision, training, and other professional tasks. Also, as salaries have gone up, and personnel costs have become an ever larger part of the cost equation, it is distinctly uneconomic to cut down on the materials—the tools—that library staff have to work with.

All types of libraries have tried to save by having businesslike budgets; by having funds available so that purchasing could be done throughout the year as materials came out and were needed; by direct purchasing from the several large publishers whose lists are big enough to enable the library to effect savings over dealing through a jobber; by buying processed materials eliminating wasteful duplicative technical services; by tapping into such centralized bibliographic and references services as those of the Ohio College Library Center; by the use of computers for ordering and circulation systems that save time and provide more efficient, user-oriented retrieval and needed material; and by the full use of inter-library loan. The widespread use of International Standard Book Numbers and Cataloging in Publication (Library of Congress) has made computerized processing much less costly and more efficient.

The cost of library materials has gone up tremendously in recent years and will undoubtedly in the present inflationary economy continue to do so. The average cost of a book in 1972 was $12.99, a 54 per cent increase over the average cost in 1967. Users' needs for more accurate and up-to-date information increases as events move more quickly and the information explosion continues. In 1960, the total output of books published was 15,012 titles (in the United States); in 1972, it was 38,053 titles. In addition, in order to become true multi-media centers, all types of libraries are having to buy, or should be able to buy, a much greater range of audio-visual materials and the equipment to use them. Further the number of periodical titles—specialized titles—is growing sharply.

With this brief look at how library money is spent, we might look briefly at all three levels from which money comes to support them: local, state, and federal. We will see that in no case does the federal investment in any type of library exceed about 9 per cent at present, and that it is indeed this 9 per cent that allows for a growing edge, for innovation, for experimentation.

It is important to remember that state and local governments have only sales and property taxes to yield them revenues in states that have no income tax.

Before the advent of the first federal aid to public libraries in 1956, public library support was for the most part an unstable, meager, and haphazard affair. Funds were provided from municipal and county revenues mostly on a catch-as-catch-can basis, from the property taxes which produce about 85 per cent of all local tax dollars. The influx of federal funds through grants to the states has broadened and regularized local support far out of proportion to the size of the federal share. The federal share of public library financing is only about 7.4 per cent; library expenditures from the states own revenue sources total about 11.7 per cent; and about 81 per cent of the total bill for public library services is financed by local governments. Money is provided mainly by municipalities, but in some states, counties, townships, and special districts contribute as much as a third of the support from their revenues.

Six or perhaps seven states had programs of direct aid to local public libraries from state resources in 1956. As of 1970–71, thirty-five states were authorized to make appropriations for state grants in aid to public libraries, but twenty-three actually did so. The total amount in those years was $52.5 million of which only nine states accounted for $45 million, or about 82 per cent of the total for all states. New York State alone appropriated $15.5 million, or about one third. In most states, the aid systems for local public libraries still operate at a very nominal level, but as of 1974, thirty-six states had appropriated a total of $81,740,000, and thirty-eight states had indicated that they would appropriate money in 1975. Several states, including Nebraska, have made it a matter of legal policy to guarantee, from state allocations, ongoing programs during periods of delayed funding, deferrals, rescissions, and the like, such as have been experienced in recent years with federal funds. In New Jersey, the budget for state aid for libraries for fiscal year 1976 has been cut 25 per cent below last year's.

There are three primary types of formulas for disbursement of state aid. Four states—California, Illinois, Michigan, and New York—use the "plan" system: they require local libraries to submit plans about how they expect to use state funds; reorganization of the library system as a separate legal entity; designation of a headquarters library that provides wide access and dissemination of services; and some local tax support.

A second model, used by Pennsylvania, Rhode Island, Massachusetts, and New Jersey, establishes several strata of libraries with regional or district level responsibility, which receive state aid accordingly. A third model, used by Maryland with great success, is a modified matching system in which the state provides a fluctuating percentage of local library revenue.

The $814 million—less than $4.00 per capita expended by states and localities for public library services in fiscal 1971–72—was less than the amount spent from local sources for virtually every other domestic service. It was about one third the amount spent for parks and recreation, and less than one sixth of the amount spent for police protection. It was also less than 2 per cent of the states' local expenditures for elementary and secondary schools.

Per capita expenditure for public libraries ranged in 1971–72 from a low of $1.58 per capita in Alabama and Arkansas, to a high of $7.76 in Massachusetts. Of course, in view of recent inflation, these dollars have probably been increased somewhat, but so equally—probably more so—has the cost of the services they buy. A really good program, one that comes close to realizing the potential of public library services for meeting the needs of users at both ends of the clientele spectrum—from the highly educated specialist to the culturally isolated slum child—costs, in 1975 a minimum of $15.00 per capita.

Since the beginning of federal support for public libraries some $560 million—more than half a billion dollars over a period of nearly twenty years—has been matched by well over a billion-dollar investment in public libraries of local and state funds. LSCA Title I—for services—has always been granted to support a very wide range of services. It has always suffered from a yawning gap between the amount authorized to do the job and the amount actually appropriated.

In fiscal 1969—five years after the revision which broadened the LSCA from purely rural responsibilities to responsibility for public libraries in all kinds of areas—the amount budgeted and spent was $35 million. The Nixon administration revised the budget downward for fiscal 1970, and attempted to cut the appropriation for Title I in half, but the heroic efforts of the Education coalition lobby (of which ALA has always been an active partner) achieved restoration in the amount of $29,800,000. Aware that public library constituents were not going to take major cuts lying down, the Administration next asked for this same amount, but the Congress funded the title—which has a lot of friends in Congress—at the $35 million level of pre-Nixon days.

Fiscal year 1972 began a new authorization for LSCA, which extends through fiscal year 1976 (June 30, 1976). The mandate for LSCA this time around calls for it to: assist states to develop and improve public library service in geographical areas and to groups of persons without adequate service; provide library services for patients and inmates of state-supported institutions directly, or by funding local libraries for this service; provide services for the physically handicapped; provide services for disadvantaged persons in low-income areas, both urban and rural; strengthen metropolitan public libraries which function as regional or national reference centers; and strengthen the capacity of the state library agency to meet the library and information needs of all the people.

Quite a job! For fiscal 1972, $112,000,000 was authorized by the Congress to accomplish it. The Administration's budget recommendation was a sour joke—in fact, an insult: $15,719,000; Congress appropriated $46,568,500. *Basic* allotment for each state, Puerto Rico, and the District of Columbia, which met state and local maintenance and other requirements was $200,000 with the balance distributed in relation to the total resident population of the state. Of the $80 million authorized by Congress for Title II of LSCA—construction—Congress appropriated some $9,500,000 providing a basic allotment of $100,000 to each state.

Appropriated, impounded, and finally released for fiscal years 1973 and 1974 together under LSCA for public libraries was $76,155,000 for services, Title I; $15 million for construction, Title II; and $7,364,000 for Interlibrary Cooperation, Title III. For fiscal year 1975, $49,155,000 for Title I, and $2,594,000 for Title III were appropriated, after attempts at deferrals and rescissions, with President Ford's signature in December 1974.

Immediately the struggle for public library money under LSCA for fiscal year 1976, began again. After the conference of House and Senate on appropriations approved funding at the same level as the previous year—a total of $51,749,000 divided between Title I and Title III—the President vetoed the appropriations bill in July 1975. The President insisted that the education appropriations bill was a "budget-buster"; many members of Congress disagreed with him, including Senator Bellmon, Republican from Oklahoma, and top Republican member of the Senate Budget Committee.

"I wish to emphasize," Senator Bellmon said, speaking of the *Senate* version of the House-Senate compromise bill —which was for some $200 million more than the vetoed version, "that this bill is not a budget-buster. The bill simply represents a rearrangement of priorities by the Congress." Many members of the Congress have made the point that the education appropriations bill was well within the fiscal year 1976 spending targets agreed to by Congress in the spring. The point of contention between the Administration and the Congress is therefore one of priorities.

Congress, it seems obvious, puts a higher priority on education (and on libraries) than does the Administration.

The fiscal year 1976 education appropriations act became public law 94-94 on September 10, 1975, following congressional override of the President's veto. The vote to override was 379 to 41 in the House, and 88 to 12 in the Senate, reflecting strong support for education and libraries in both Houses of Congress. In short, the Congress remained determined to reorder the Administration's budget priorities. Further, despite an earlier message transmitted to Congress proposing rescissions and deferrals, the funds were to be sent out from the Office of Education, as appropriated, before the end of the calendar year 1975. Thus public and higher education library programs—with funds for fiscal 1976 of $51,749,000 and $18,975,000 respectively once again narrowly escaped severe cuts. "Carry-over funds" to take care of the three-month gap to be created with the changeover of the fiscal year (fiscal 1977 is scheduled to begin October 1, 1976, instead of July 1) were still being sought as this book went to press.

Turning now to federal funding for college library resources, let's take a look at what has happened to that picture in the recent past, and present.

Between 1969 and 1971, funds for college libraries were decreased on the President's recommendation by some 76 per cent. HEA II, parts A and B, were among the first to feel the most drastic effects of the President's efforts to "phase out" special library funding. Authorization for the act, enacted in 1965, extends at present through fiscal year 1975—which means that at this writing it is up for extension or amendment. While direct dollar amounts for grants to institutions for their college library resources have always been small, they have been a real godsend to eligible colleges and universities. And from Title II B, with its two sections which cover training for library staff on the one hand, and research and demonstration on the other, have come some of the most innovative and replicatable of all programs for today's libraries of all types.

The total appropriation for HEA II for fiscal year 1972,

for example, was $15,750,000 ($11,000,000 for Part A; $2,000,000 for Part B-Training; and $2,750,000 for research. For fiscal year 1973 Part A received $12,500,000; Part B-Training $3,572,000, and Part B-Research and Demonstration, only $1,785,000. HEA 1973 funds escaped impoundment, incidentally.

Like all other library programs, the Administration's budget request for fiscal year 1974 attempted to "zero" out HEA II completely, but Congress appropriated $14,250,000 (after the allowable 5 per cent presidential cut, the price of passage that year). After threatened rescissions had been turned back, funding for HEA Title II surfaced for fiscal year 1975 at $9,975,000 for Part A, and $3 million for Part B.

Actually a number of college libraries, especially community colleges that are starting out, received significant sums of money from Title III of HEA for Developing Institutions, funded for $87,492,000 in fiscal year 1973; for $99,992,000 in fiscal year 1974, and for $110,000,000 for 1975. They received money also from the Post-Secondary Education Fund, under which authorization $10 million was appropriated for the first time in 1973. From the latter, such diverse institutions as the University of Montana at Missoula, and the Community College of Vermont at Montpelier, received $49,378 and $750,548 respectively to establish library-learning opportunities in non-traditional settings for isolated rural residents.

College libraries have also received some monies under HEA VI which provides undergraduate materials and equipment, and this past fiscal year (1975) funded for $7,500,000; while the Post-Secondary Education fund rose in fiscal year 1975 to an appropriation of $15 million.

Where do federal funds for college libraries go from here? And how about the small but terribly critical amounts for training and for research and for demonstration? The Higher Education programs which expired June 30, 1975, have been extended for one additional year, to give Congress time to complete work on Higher Education Amendments. Both House and Senate bills recommended $9,975,000 for Part A of HEA II—exactly the same amount as last year—as against the Administration's zero budget request for Part A. The conference committee, however, proposed only $1,500,000 to be divided between the two sections of Part B—again substituting for the Administration's zero request. Part B would realize only a pitiful half of its already tiny 1975 appropriation, and the amount allocated for training has dwindled to only $500,000.

As in the case of LSCA, success by the Congress in overriding the President's veto of the fiscal year 1976 appropriations bill meant a reprieve for Higher Education library programs. In a time when state governments are as squeezed as they are, the chance of more funding coming through the states to state institutions and land-grant colleges seems slim, and many privately supported colleges are only too close to having to close their doors altogether, let alone their libraries. There are virtually no reliable or compatible figures for college libraries, as there are for public and even school libraries, to show what proportions of their support come from state, as compared with federal, sources.

The National Program for Acquisitions and Cataloging (HEA II C) which is now carried on under the authority of the Library of Congress, will henceforth be funded through the legislative-branch appropriations bill which for fiscal year 1976 provides $9,653,391 for it. Since the former HEA II C need not then be extended, the ALA has suggested that a new Part C be added to HEA II which would provide a new authority to assist research libraries, such as that proposed by the Carnegie Council on Higher Education. A report of Carnegie Council deliberations states:

> We believe that the Federal government should inaugurate a program of financial support for large research libraries. Allocations would be based on such factors as numbers of doctoral degrees awarded and Federal support of academic

science in each institution. Some consideration should be given also in the allocation process to a reasonable regional balance in the availability of funds.

The Carnegie Council recommends initial funding of such a program at the level of $10 million.

In endorsing the Carnegie proposal, ALA stated in testimony submitted to the Senate Subcommittee on Education —which held hearings both before and after the congressional August recess—that it should not be tied to the numbers of Ph.D. degrees granted, "because this would eliminate the major urban public libraries as well as an institution like the Research Libraries of the N. Y. Public Library which do not grant degrees but which house some of the great research collections of the nation." ALA also recommended that applicants for such research library grants should not be also eligible to apply for the HEA II A basic grants (of $5,000).

Hearings of the Senate Subcommittee on Education under Chairman Claiborne Pell were for the purpose of seeking information on how federal higher-education programs are operating, and what can be done to improve them. ALA submitted testimony also emphasizing that the programs authorized under HEA II A and B are more vital than ever "because of changing patterns of enrollment, sky-rocketing costs for books and magazines, new concepts of information retrieval, and a growing demand for librarians skilled in working with the handicapped and disadvantaged."

Citing the Administration's opposition to funding HEA I programs over several recent years on the one hand, and striking similarities between the existing HEA II B demonstration program and the Administration's proposed Library Partnership Act on the other, ALA suggested to the Senate subcommittee that they consider incorporating parts of the partnership proposal within HEA II B, since: "Eligible activities under an expanded Title II B program would be much as they are now under the existing program—demonstrations designed to encourage exemplary and innovative developments in the provision of library and information services, and programs with special emphasis on improvements which benefit disadvantaged groups, such as the partnership act proposes, and also a variety of forms of training and retraining of library personnel such as are now provided under HEA II B."

And so we come to school media centers—those libraries whose fortunes are so inextricably tied up with those of the school systems they serve. With ever mounting criticism of the local tax base as the chief arbiter of educational opportunity—and ever more taxpayer revolts, as property taxes mount—the federal portion of funds that have brought school library media programs to their present level of effectiveness looms ever more important.

Beginning with state allocations, a few illustrations are illuminating. In Maryland, for the 1973–74 school year, an allocation of $5.10 per pupil for materials only is lumped under the state-aid formula for education; another $12.26 is allocated for textbooks, and approximately another $7.00 per pupil for equipment and other consumable items, makes a total portion of about $25 per pupil from the over-all state aid monies allocated for library media programs.

The state of Connecticut returns a flat reimbursement grant of $250 per pupil to each school district by way of state school aid, but the Board of Education must gain permission of the Board of Finance to use the money for school purposes so it must be considered as replacement for, not funds in addition to, local support.

In the state of Ohio, the average annual expenditure for books and all other materials such as media kits, films, slides, etc. per child was $3.88. There are some 620 public school districts, which operate a total of 4,213 school buildings, of which 1,716 have central libraries; of the state's 846 private schools, 265 have central libraries. Total public school expenditure for all library materials and equipment was (the latest figures) $9,500,000 including both local and federal sources; $3 million was spent by the private schools.

In Fulton County, Ohio, figures for the 1971–72 school year show that with an enrollment of 8,915 pupils and only 3 certified librarians, the amount spent in local funds for library media (including books, periodicals, microforms, newspapers and AV) was $32,991; an additional amount of $13,541 in federal funds brought the total to $46,532, or $5.21 per pupil for library instructional materials.

Contrast this with the Stamford, Connecticut, public schools—17 of them elementary, 4 middle schools, and 3 high schools—all of which have centralized media centers and professionally conducted programs. The total school enrollment is 20,000 pupils, and $250,000 a year is spent on the materials and equipment for the media program (not including salaries or capital expenditures) for an allocation per capita of $12.50 per child. Of this, Title II of ESEA supplies about $18,000 for the use of the children in the public schools and about $7,000 for use of the children in the private, or independent, schools, of whom there are 4,100.

The support situation is, to say the least, uneven. This bears out the findings of a survey of State School Library-Media Supervisors, undertaken in May 1974 by the Legislation Committee of the American Association of School Librarians. From the responses it can be said that a majority of the states rely on a combination of local and state funding, and several rather more heavily than others on ESEA II, Vocational Education Act, Title I of ESEA and other federal titles. Some states reported the granting of one-time assistance to school districts in the event that federal funds were eliminated or deferred; others mentioned special levies or private fund sources to supplement state aid. Forty-eight state supervisors reported that school library funding was basically the responsibility of the local education agency; forty-four said that funds were raised by district/local taxes, and thirty-three by general state aid. Only eleven supervisors said that their states provided specific subsidies for school library support; some examples from the survey responses include: Louisiana state law (from 1936) allocates $1.00 per pupil from state funds, with additional responsibility that of the local education agency; North Carolina allocates $8.00 per capita for instructional materials and supplies; Utah provides $500,000 per year to schools for media support; Wisconsin, $1.23 per capita, with local education agencies required to spend more than this. Tennessee provides for school library-media programs $2.00 per capita based on average daily attendance; and Massachusetts has a law authorizing a state subsidy, but no appropriation of funds. In Hawaii, all schools are state-funded, and the amount allocated for library purposes is determined by individual school principals.

And so to the question of federal funds for school media and library needs. Only in the first year of funding —fiscal year 1966 which began July 1, 1965—has the full amount authorized under Title II of ESEA been appropriated: $100 million. Although the authorization under the act had risen to well over $200 million by fiscal year 1973, only $90 million had been appropriated and this had been partially impounded by the President, who refused to release it for spending, along with funds under Title III of NDEA. It was, as we have said, released later. Authorization for ESEA as well as NDEA ran out at the end of fiscal 1973 (June 30 of that year) and Congress provided a contingency authorization, and an appropriation, for fiscal 1974. The ESEA Title II appropriation was for $90,250,000; NDEA Title III was appropriated at the level of $26,250,000.

In August of 1974, President Ford signed the Education Amendments of 1974 (HR 69). The new amendments provided for a phased-in consolidation of the school library resources program (ESEA II) with educational equipment (NDEA III) *and* the part of ESEA III which relates to testing, counseling, and guidance. These components constitute a new title to be known as ESEA IV, Part B: Libraries and Learning Resources. Part C of this same title (ESEA IV) deals with that part of the former ESEA III that concerned Supplementary Educational Centers and Services, and includes also the former ESEA Title V (strengthening state and local educational agencies) and other sections of ESEA that have to do with dropout prevention, and demonstration projects to improve school nutrition and health services for the children of low-income families.

It is important to note that this new ESEA Title IV can take effect only if, in any given year, certain conditions are met. The conditions are:

1) there must be forward funding—that is, appropriations for the consolidated programs must be enacted a year in advance;

2) appropriations for the consolidated programs for any given year must be no less than the fiscal year 1974 level, or the level of the preceding year, whichever is higher.

This does *not* insure, however, that school library media programs are certain of receiving amounts equal to what they received under the previous titles, since this allocation is at the discretion of the state education agency. Some degree of protection is afforded to school libraries by the fact that since ESEA II is extended through fiscal year 1978, the school library media program is still authorized in its pre-consolidation form, should the conditions for consolidation not be met in any year. But in any year in which consolidation conditions are met, the school library media program must be authorized under the new ESEA IV.

Meanwhile, the HEW appropriations act signed by President Ford in December 1974 provided funds for fiscal year 1975 for ESEA Title II in the amount of $95,250,000, and for NDEA III in the amount of $21,750,000. This was to be the final year of these two titles, before the beginning of consolidation into the new ESEA IV B. Also, so that the phase-in of the new title could begin on July 1, 1975 (the beginning of fiscal year 1976) the forward funding was also included in the amount of $137,330,000, to be allocated, in this first phase-in year *half* to the former separate library, guidance materials, and equipment and media titles, and *half* to the new Title IV B, which consolidates them all.

What this means is that school library media programs would *surely* receive, between July 1, 1975, and June 30, 1976, $45,125,000 from the old ESEA II, and $14,125,000 from the old NDEA III. *In addition,* they would be expected to see to it that they got their fair share for school library programs of the $68,665,000 that was appropriated for fiscal year 1976 to ESEA IV Part B.

Perhaps an illustration with specific figures would be helpful. The following is for the state of Connecticut:

Elementary and Secondary Media Funding

Fiscal year 1975 (1974–75 school year)
NDEA III $ 202,360
ESEA II $1,349,182

Fiscal year 1976 (1975–76 school year)
NDEA III $ 145,091
ESEA II $ 686,953
Guidance
(ESEA III) $ 126,357

ESEA IV B $ 978,053   (can be spent in mandated areas in any proportion desired by the local education agency)

Fiscal year 1977 (1976–77 school year)
ESEA IV B $2,462,588   (can be spent in mandated areas in any proportion desired by the local education agency)

An amendment offered during the debate over the education appropriations bill for fiscal year 1976 added an additional $10,000,000 to the forward funding of ESEA IV B for fiscal year 1977, when it will become the total replacement for the former titles. This was a part of the bill vetoed by the President late in July and passed by

Congress over his veto. Fiscal year 1977 funding for Title IV B is $147,330,000.

The Congress has shown great concern for providing adequate federal support for school library media centers and programs. John Brademas, Democrat from Indiana's Third Congressional District and Chairman of the House Select Committee on Education, in a National Library Week statement to members of the House on April 18, 1975, paid tribute to all the nation's libraries, and discussed in some detail his concern, and that of the subcommittee, "that if the program does not work as Congress intends, we will want to know." He was talking of the new ESEA IV B.

"This new program, if adequately funded a year in advance, in accordance with the provisions of the authorizing legislation—Public Law 93-380—will replace three existing categorical programs: Title II of ESEA which provides grants for school library resources; Title III of NDEA which provides grants for the acquisition of educational equipment and minor remodeling; and part of Title III of ESEA which is for guidance, counseling and testing. The new consolidated Title IV B of ESEA is designed to provide local school districts with more flexibility in the use of Federal education funds for these purposes . . .

"When any new program takes effect, there is uncertainty as to how it will work, and the new ESEA is no exception . . . We in Congress, and particularly those of us on the Education and Labor Committee are fully aware that there will be some problems in changing from individual programs to the new consolidated one, but we feel confident that once the transition is made, the new program will be a worthy successor to the highly successful individual categorical programs it is designed to replace . . . Mr. Speaker, as we make the transition to the new Title IV program, I want the record to be clear on one point. We in Congress will be watching closely as the consolidated libraries and learning resources takes effect, 50% in fiscal 1976, and completely in fiscal year 1977. If there are problems, we will want to know about them."

If school media specialists are as skillful, as knowledgeable, as eclectic about the learning program and the curriculum, and as watchful and energetic as they have been in the past, they should have little trouble making the new ESEA IV B work well for the continuing development of school library media programs.

And that is how it was with money for libraries in fall of 1975—uncertain, up in the air, but on the whole hopeful. But librarians had learned, by and large, to take it as it came, to roll with the punches, and never to call it quits because they knew that no other agencies could do as well what they could do if they had the means—and they knew that lots of other people knew it too. It is to be hoped, though, they had learned something else as well: that they would be better off in future if they took some initiatives and planned ahead, so that they could control, in some degree at least, the punches they had to roll with!

Chapter VI: Library Futures—Purpose and Resources

The last quarter of the century, the last moments, indeed, of the millennium, have begun with higher expectations, and more demands of libraries, than they have ever known before. They bring with them though, these expectations and demands, many questions and as yet not very many answers.

What are the purposes, the goals, and the objectives of library-media-information-learning resource centers to be? What kinds of structures, what courses of action will make possible the achievement of the goals that are selected, and how does one know when they are being achieved? What kind of priorities must be set among the many objectives, and how to arrive at a consensus about them? And where should the money come from to carry out the programs?

It would be impossible to describe even briefly, let alone discuss fully, all of the studies, the recommendations relative to future directions which have emerged during the past decade—to say nothing of all that went before. One can only synthesize and hope perhaps to summarize, where all the thinking, the writing, and the talking seem to have arrived by the summer of 1975, and identify a few of the idea carriers, some of the main streams that have fed into the present corporate wisdom.

The times themselves, the social and economic climate, have been a galvanizing factor—as always with libraries. The instability of the economy has brought new awareness and spurred the decision-making process. As cities and states look hard at their priorities among many services they cannot pay for, all types of libraries are being forced to know, and be able to explain clearly why they are cost-effective, and why they should be maintained out of shrinking local and state revenues; and as the nation slides ever deeper into debt and deficit spending, they must be able to request of Congress money that makes sense in terms of co-ordinated library services.

We will begin the review—or the preview—of things to come with the opinions of librarians themselves, and at the national level with their chief professional organizational representative, the American Library Association. It is, as it has always been, the librarians' responsibility to lead, to forge the path for their own profession, and spell out its responsibilities and develop some means of carrying them out. This means, as it has always meant for leaders, *listening:* listening to the needs of users, listening to and involving others who must be involved in the enterprise.

We talk a great deal now in plans and projections about "user needs" and the semantics here are important. Many people seem to equate "needs" with "demands" for library service, but they are not always synonymous. In planning for libraries to meet "user needs" we must consider the unperceived, the unstated, even the unconscious needs of people as well as those which have been actually transformed into demand. This transformation process might be expressed: NEED equals Necessity Explored, Expressed, Developed, and then leading to Demand. Real needs often go unexpressed if they are thought to be unrealistic, or incapable of realization. People must first believe that their needs can be met, and for those with many lacks, it is often difficult to pinpoint a specific need and sufficiently enlarge the perception of it to get at basic root causes. It must then all be put into the proper "retrieval terms" if help is to be obtained. Demands of libraries are educated needs, but it is not only the undereducated who have trouble "getting at" and expressing what they really want.

After several years of disjointedness, internal conflict, economic peril, and agonizing reappraisal, the ALA, by '75, had emerged nearly whole again and solvent. It had been blessed with a strong executive director in Robert Wedgeworth and a leadership apparatus and membership convinced once again that it could work, and willing to make it a constructive instrument. Many reports and committees preceded the new expression of goals and objectives for the association which was approved at the midwinter business meeting in January 1975. All units of the ALA have now begun writing long-range plans that insure that the course of future activity of all divisions and committees and other units will be consonant with the over-all thrust, and that the entire association will move in the same direction.

The goals and objectives by which the organized profession of librarianship will be guided—subject to continuous evaluation and revision—during the next few years are as follows:

"The goal of the American Library Association is the promotion of libraries and librarianship to assure the delivery of user-oriented library and information services to all."

More about this user-orientation a little later, but it is interesting to note here that it was the Executive Board of ALA that inserted this phrase in the final draft that was brought to it for approval. It is an important footnote too, that "information" as used here "includes not only facts and data, but ideas and the products of man's creative endeavors" and his experience and wisdom. School media specialists have defined information in their recently published guidelines as being: "all sensory input."

Five objectives were also adopted as guides to future decision-making, and with the intention of shaping decisions geared to the goal. They follow:

1. Provision of information services and resources for all the people of the United States of America, in order to increase their opportunity to participate in society, to learn, to achieve self-fulfillment, to pursue careers, and to obtain information needed for research.

2. Provision of leadership for interlibrary co-operation leading to a nation-wide information delivery system which equalizes access to information resources.

3. Cooperation to achieve increased access to library and information resources throughout the world.

4. Support of intellectual freedom as expressed in the "Library Bill of Rights" and "The Freedom to Read" statement, and support of librarians, trustees or libraries whose defense of these principles is challenged.

5. Development and support of library personnel through affirmative action, education, personal welfare, and training.

Implementary steps, a course of action toward these objectives have been spelled out too. They include:

A. Coordinating with other appropriate organizations as their goals and activities relate to those of ALA, such as: governmental agencies; the information industry; international bodies; learned, professional and scientific societies; mass media; publishers; social service agencies.

B. Developing effective legislative programs at all levels of government to: assure that laws on copyright, government documents, public information, communication technology, and other concerns facilitate and extend library service; and provide appropriate statutory bases.

C. Establishing guidelines and/or standards for: employment status and welfare of librarians; equalization of service to users regardless of socio-economic status, location, handicaps and other conditions; interlibrary cooperation; organization of collections for access; physical facilities and equipment; professional education and training for library personnel; scope and quality of collections and services; utilization of emerging technologies.

D. Evaluating programs in terms of guidelines and stated objectives to assure accountability and to measure progress.

E. Investigating and making facts known, providing testimony, filing briefs, and other appropriate legal actions.

F. Mobilizing a vigorous public relations program in behalf of libraries and library services.

G. Providing a vehicle for discussion and action on socially sensitive issues related to library service.

H. Sponsoring publications, conferences, orientation programs, workshops and so forth.

I. Stimulating and coordinating research including but not limited to areas of development, organization and use of resources, networks, planning and evaluation, management freedom and personnel.

J. Strengthening and encouraging ALA chapters to work effectively in accomplishment of ALA's Goals and Objectives.

These professional objectives have grown out of numerous group and individual self-searching efforts. Outstanding among them in its clarity and organization, as well as for its applicability to all types of libraries—although it is addressed primarily to public libraries—was the study of proposed public library goals, *A Strategy for Public Library Change,* co-ordinated and written by Allie Beth Martin, librarian of the Tulsa City-County Library in Oklahoma, and president of the American Library Association from July 1975 through the annual conference marking the association's centennial in 1976.

Published in 1972 by ALA, the study showed that some of the problems that were uppermost in the minds of the more than 200 library leaders questioned or interviewed concerning public libraries could be said to be problems of school and college librarians as well. They included: problems related to finance; management problems; failure to formulate objectives; failure to serve all publics; staff inflexibility and lack of user-orientation; initial and continuing professional education; inability to measure performance; failure to integrate all media and to utilize technology to the fullest; and lack of interlibrary co-operation.

Strategy cited two divergent viewpoints among the librarians queried. One outlook, rejected by the majority of respondents, Mrs. Martin characterized as the "prophet of doom" response, according to which the public library would soon become extinct and be replaced. The other viewpoint about the future was "characterized by a spirit of hope, a sense of the future which will require libraries, or some other similar institution more than ever before. The proponents of this philosophy say librarians will become active agents serving the needs of society in positive, dynamic fashion. The advocates of this point of view are enthusiastic, even excited, about the future. They temper their optimism with the realization that marked change must take place if the bright future projected is to be realized."

"The optimistic outlook," says Mrs. Martin, "is eloquently summarized by Virginia H. Mathews and Dan Lacy in their statement on "Library Responsibilities in the Next Decade" in their study, *Response to Change: American Libraries in the Seventies:*

> In summary, we can perhaps identify several principal and priority responsibilities for libraries in the next decade:
> 1. To support and sustain formal education from pre-kindergarten through graduate school, for which millions of students, widely diversified as to abilities, and goals, will require access to a greater range of media than ever before;
> 2. To play an initiatory role, with other agencies and institutions, in developing in people an

orderly acceptance of change and in helping
them to adapt to it;

3. To serve as both motivator and supplier of
aspirations for the dispossessed and disorganized;

4. To support the increasingly complex operations of government, of science, and of the business sector of the country;

5. To provide support, with and through other
agencies, of continuing self-education and training for people at all levels of work;

6. To accept the individual as an individual
and to provide spiritual nourishment, intellectual
stimulation, cultural enrichment and information
alternatives to him at the neighborhood or community level.

Finally, the *Strategy* study outlined a plan of action to
meet the requirements of users and help solve the problems librarians encounter in doing so: a public information
program; co-ordinated research and investigation to study,
among other things present users and non-users, information needs and supply, budgets and funding, professional
education and library operations; dissemination of research
findings and development of prototypes and applications in
real life through demonstrations and models; and an intensive and continuous educational effort "to insure practi-
tioners prepared to meet the constant challenge of
change." Among librarians, there is a critical need to
know, says Mrs. Martin:

How to determine the library and information
needs of each community
How to develop plans—set goals—*with* not *for*
users
How to communicate what the library is doing
so that it becomes truly visible
How to manage libraries so effectively that they
will receive needed support

How to perform actively, not passively
How to change and help others to change

Typical of many other creative endeavors to "think through" some of the problems of change, service, and cost-effectiveness is the report of a conference sponsored by the Joint Committee of the American Library Association and the National Education Association to develop and rationalize some thinking about the possibilities of *Total Community Library Service,* published also in 1972. There was "unanimous agreement among conference participants that planning for library services, now and in the future, must involve all of the interested agencies, and that coordination of activities, services, resources and even facilities is not only feasible but desirable depending upon the needs of the community to be served." The discussion concerned a multi-agency approach to library service, and some implications for community library service emerged from the papers and discussions.

> Community libraries are obviously something more than supplementary education centers; they are centers in which considerable teaching and learning takes place, of both a formal and informal nature. In planning the kinds of services the library is to provide, this educative function should be central, not incidental. . . .
>
> Consideration of the community library's education role might include attention to the library as an extension of the home and neighborhood. For example, during the critical early childhood years, the library can contribute to the cognitive and affective growth of children as well as to parental, home and family education.

Recommendations from this report included the development of models and pilot projects involving the co-ordination of school, public and other library services at the community level; exploration of the concepts of a community co-ordinating council charged with co-ordination of a community system of library and learning resources; and high priority accorded to the development of "impact indicators" and evaluation tools that could measure and contrast the effectiveness of various patterns of service. "Market research" to ascertain user needs, continuing education and retraining of professionals, full use of all media, print and non-print, appropriate legislation, and more user involvement in program planning were again reflected as priority requirements if a decent job were to be done.

School library media specialists and college librarians, as specialized clientele professionals, have spelled out goals for service to their constituents.

In *Media Programs: District and School*, published in 1975, the American Association of School Librarians joined with the Association for Educational Communications and Technology the functions, purposes and operation of the media program within the schools. The statements are direct and specific: "The media program exists to support and further the purposes formulated by the school or district of which it is an integral part, and its quality is judged by its effectiveness in achieving program purposes. A media program represents a combination of resources that includes people, materials, machines, facilities and environments, as well as purposes and processes."

Media Programs goes on to say that "activities of the media program should be considered in the light of four functions: *design, consultation, information* and *administration.* . . . The design function relates to formulating and analyzing objectives; establishing priorities; developing or identifying alternatives; selecting among alternatives; and implementing and evaluating the system, the product, the strategy, or technique. . . . The consultation function is applied as media professionals contribute to the identification of teaching and learning strategies; work with teachers and students in the evaluation, selection and production of materials; and serve as consultants in planning and reordering physical facilities to provide effective learning environments. . . . The information function relates especially to providing sources and services appropriate to user needs and devising delivery systems of materials, tools and human resources to provide for maximum access to information in all its forms. . . . The administration function is concerned with the ways and means by which program goals and priorities are achieved." As of now, the school library-media professionals have probably done the best and most thorough job of defining their responsibilities.

There is little question that school and college libraries, geared directly and inextricably to the needs of students—and further, students who function in a more or less structured learning environment—have, at present, a somewhat less complex job of defining their responsibilities than do public libraries. But what of community schools, scattered-site education, and other proposals? To be sure the student population, whether at elementary, secondary, or post-secondary level runs the gamut of abilities, interests, styles, and needs; none the less, the school or college library can narrow and focus its services in some degree. Also, in terms of funding, school libraries are at least tied to the fortunes—for good or ill—of institutions larger than themselves, while public libraries run in poor competition to them, and to a variety of other services, for funding. But what of the states, which now by law must find alternatives to property-tax-based, and inherently unequal, education? School and college libraries, more than ever, are in constant need of interpreting their roles, proving their productivity and fighting for their budgets within the institutional budget.

A study made possible by a fellowship from the Council on Library Resources was conducted in 1974 to survey some examples of goal and objectives setting efforts as part of management activity in selected large public libraries. Mr. Larry Earl Bone, library director at Southwestern University at Memphis, Tennessee, found that a number of large libraries either had, or were in process of setting themselves some objectives and struggling to sort out priorities, among them: Brooklyn, Baltimore, Chicago, Dallas, Denver, Detroit, Minneapolis, Memphis, New York, Philadelphia, Pittsburgh, Tulsa, Seattle, and Washington, D.C.

It is interesting to note that those that seem to be the furthest along in the process were not the very largest, but those in Dallas, Denver, Memphis, Minneapolis, and Tulsa —which seems to suggest that perhaps it is easier for libraries of this size to identify and define their missions than for those in the larger cities.

Mr. Bone cites different methods for arriving at the goals and objectives: large committees with task forces; small committees; workshops. Those processes which involved library staff at all levels seem to have been most successful. "One can conclude," he says, "that no goals and objectives will ever be successfully implemented unless the library staff as a whole becomes involved . . . staff resistance to the changes brought about by new goals and objectives may be strong unless general involvement is achieved." He cites Tulsa and Dallas as libraries where the greatest number of staff have participated, and as being those where considerable enthusiasm has been generated. He makes the point, illustrated by the Memphis experience, that if only top-level staff takes part, it may take more time to make the objectives a reality. If only middle or lower staff take part, goals may lack vision, as Minneapolis found.

Community involvement, the researcher found, has been minimal in almost all of the libraries that have undertaken these assessments, with the exceptions of Washington and Tulsa. He cites also a lack of community analysis—assessments of user need—before goals are set.

Community analysis is an active concern with Denver, and the Memphis Public Library has quite deliberately involved the community with a recent revision of its earlier objectives. Sometimes, Mr. Bone learned—and it certainly stands to reason—political considerations make it difficult, if not impossible, to make clear-cut decisions about objectives, let alone identify priorities—with the accompanying necessity to make cuts in non-priority areas. And many big city library directors—in New York and Philadelphia, for example—feel that any objective setting remains a fairly futile exercise in the present climate of crisis management and unstable finances which prevent creative long-range planning.

However, it is interesting to note that clear-cut and very visible priorities have been set by the Denver system, in Detroit and in Memphis, which have actually helped those cities to "tap into" additional sources of federal funding beyond the library titles. Denver has chosen to focus on the needs of the adult independent learner, not only through the CLEP program (College Level Examination Program) but in other and more general culturally oriented programs which feature not only independent, self-directed study but group study experiences such as discussions, exhibits, and field trips.

Detroit's priority is unequivocally information and referral service, which operates out of the central library and the branches. Called TIP—The Information Place—Detroit's priority service required restructuring and retraining of staff and some cutting of other positions and services. But Clara Jones, director of the library (who is to be the 1976–77 president of ALA) believes wholeheartedly that institutional change that will make the library more relevant to the daily lives of people—including many who never used libraries before—is the path to survival—not only for the library, but for the society it serves.

The Memphis Public Library, whose priorities include both support for the adult independent learner and information and referral service, has been able to obtain both revenue sharing funds for its community information service, and other federal funds for adult education for its adult basic education pilot project.

Tulsa has priorities that include outreach services to the aged, institutionalized, and handicapped; the adult learner; and heightening the role of the library as a cultural and humanistic studies center of the community. Tulsa has been especially imaginative in tapping local, state, and federal monies not labeled "library" and has received several successive grants for pilot projects and ongoing programs from the National Endowment for the Humanities.

All of which points up that public libraries especially, but all libraries in fact, must do some immediate self-study to find out exactly—tradition and nostalgia aside—what they are good for, and why they should be supported, so that they will be ready with some precise and cogent answers—we hope some irrefutable answers—when the challenge comes. The field abounds in intelligent, thoughtful people with sound and creative ideas about what libraries should be doing; what is needed is a framework for their thinking and an organized rationalization process for making use of it.

In a speech, "Media in Libraries—Luxury or Necessity?" Dr. Estelle Jussim, professor in the School of Library Science at Simmons College in Boston poses some challenges to the media sophistication of a group of Massachusetts librarians.

> *Step 1*—Read, study, and think about David Sohn's interview with Jerzy Kosinski, published under the title "A Nation of Videots" in the April 1975 issue of *Media and Methods*. Decide, once and for all, to investigate current research findings on the passivity of students, their inability to become involved in real actions, their preference for the mediated experience over the real experience, their low frustration level and their poor self-image. Compare Kosinski's comments with David Riesman's in his famous chapter called "The Socializing Influence of Print," particularly where Riesman calls attention to the inner-directed child who believes he or she is a failure when he cannot measure up to the image of great people as presented in biographies.

> *Step 2*—Read, study and think about the First Amendment, the Red Lion Case, the deci-

sions of the Supreme Court over public access, the Sloan Commission report on cable television. Decide, once and for all, to study the corporate structure of mass communications in America.

Step 3—Make an intensive study of your community. How many newspapers are available and what is their editorial policy? Who owns the newspapers and the local radio stations? What connection do local stations have with national networks? When you have these answers, write up your analysis objectively and place it in a conspicuous location in your library.

Step 4—Decide, once and for all, that the public library is the last bastion of individual, unforced, free choice of information and experience, and that it may be the only corrective left —in an institutional sense—to the great economic monoliths of the mass broadcasters, publishers, and databank corporations. Then examine your own selection policies to determine if you really are providing alternative views, the widest possible spread of opinion, or are simply catering to the safe conformity of your local society.

Dr. Jassim closes her talk with a plea for "a flexible, pragmatic, and unprejudiced attitude which will permit us to face the technological realities of this century with optimism and courage, . . . and a profound appreciation of the political, economic, psychosocial complexities of the mass media environment . . . Quite obviously too, if cooperation among types of libraries is anathema to us for political or other reasons, then we cannot solve the financial problems implicit in our isolated status."

And so it is evident that librarians as individuals and in groups are considering new patterns for a total information and library resource. They will hammer out proposals for funding those patterns and structures while keeping the purpose of them clearly in mind, and keep presenting them, revising and presenting them again, to the Congress, the states and the local governments for the next few years.

ALA Executive Director Bob Wedgeworth said it well during his report to the annual conference of ALA in the summer of 1975: "We must join together in designing our own jobs and our own future. If we do not, somebody else is going to do it for us, and we may not be pleased with the results."

While librarians and the library professional organization have been studying future directions for library and information services, a national program has been conceived and evolved by the National Commission on Libraries and Information Science. What is this commission and who are its members?

In Chapter III it was mentioned that in 1968 a National Advisory Commission of citizens appointed by President Johnson made its report to the Administration; it then went out of business, as it was supposed to do. The report made five recommendations:

1. Establishment of a National Commission on Libraries and Information Science as a continuing federal planning agency.

2. Recognition and strengthening of the role of the Library of Congress as the National Library of the United States, and establishment of a board of advisers.

3. Establishment of a Federal Institute of Library and Information Science as a principal center for basic and applied research in all relevant areas.

4. Recognition and full acceptance of the critically important role the U. S. Office of Education currently plays in meeting needs for library services.

5. Strengthening state library agencies to overcome deficiencies in fulfilling their current functions.

The Advisory Commission had studied exhaustively the then current needs and future needs, strengths and weaknesses of library services as they existed, "leaving the members with the absolute conviction that the goal of library adequacy will be achieved only as a consequence of long-range planning and fostering of the evolutionary process of library development." The Advisory Commission proposed that the permanent commission "be charged with the responsibility of preparing full scale plans to deal with the nation's library and information needs, and for advising the Federal government and other agencies, institutions and groups—both public and private, with respect to those needs."

And so it came to pass, and Public Law 91-345 of July 1970 established The National Commission on Libraries and Information Science, as "an independent agency within the Executive Branch, with the Department of Health, Education and Welfare providing the Commission with necessary administrative services." The commission was to have "primary responsibility for developing or recommending over-all plans for carrying out the policy (stated in full on p. 104) that library and information services adequate to meet the needs of the people of the United States are essential to achieve national goals . . ."

The commission's functions are:

1. To advise the President and the Congress on the implementation of national policy by such statements, presentations and reports as it deems appropriate;

2. To conduct studies, surveys and analysis of the library and informational needs of the nation, including the special library and informational needs of rural areas, of economically, socially or culturally deprived persons, and of elderly persons, and the means by which these needs may be met through information centers, through the libraries of elementary and secondary schools and institutions of higher education,

and through public, research, special and other types of libraries;

3. To appraise the adequacies and deficiencies of current library and information resources and services, and evaluate the effectiveness of current library and information science programs;

4. To develop overall plans for meeting national library and information science needs and for the coordination of activities at the Federal, state and local levels, taking into consideration all of the library and information resources of the nation to meet those needs;

5. To be authorized to advise Federal, state, local and private agencies regarding library and information sciences;

6. To promote research and development activities which will extend and improve the Nation's library and information handling capability as essential links in the national communications network;

7. To submit to the President and the Congress (not later than January 31st of each year) a report on its activities during the preceding fiscal year; and

8. To make and publish such additional reports as it deems to be necessary, including but not limited to, reports of consultants, transcripts of testimony, summary reports and reports of other Commission findings, studies and recommendations.

The NCLIS was further authorized to contract with federal agencies and public and private agencies to carry out its functions; conduct hearings; and the heads of all federal agencies are, to the extent not prohibited by law, directed to co-operate with the commission in carrying out the purposes of the act.

The NCLIS got off to a slow start as a result of tardy appointment of membership and staff, and some uncertainties about the extent of its authority and direction. Members decided that they needed updated knowledge about the library conditions of the nation, and accordingly held hearings in various regions of the country during 1972 and early 1973. They were struck by the increasing diversity of needs. During its first two years of active life, the commission also set in motion studies, and a conference at Denver, on the specialized information needs of certain groups of users (or potential users) in relation to those of the society as a whole; let a contract to study public library financing and make recommendations concerning alternative patterns; made a report, with recommendations concerning the Library of Congress; sponsored a study of bibliographic and resource centers; launched a study on the retraining and continuing education of librarians and other library workers; and endorsed and began to draw up preliminary plans for the White House Conference on Libraries and Information Science.

In June of 1973, the NCLIS voted to direct its total energies toward the preparation of the draft of a National Program for Library and Information Science—a program that would provide the base for the new federal legislation the commission expects to recommend starting in 1976. After two years, and at least three drafts which were widely circulated and criticized by the library community, officials and members of the information-using and information-producing publics, the commission produced its *Goals for Action: Toward a National Program for Library and Information Science.*

The ALA, meeting in San Francisco in July of 1975 became, appropriately, the first national organization to officially support the NCLIS program plan. It went on record expressing, "appreciation to the NCLIS for its leadership in producing this document," and voted that "the ALA concur in concepts and recommendations contained in the report and commit ALA and its units to maximum cooperation with NCLIS in implementation and further development of the Goals for Action."

The commission's goal is "to develop a plan for a flexible network of information services to meet the immediate and foreseeable information requirements of the greatest possible number of people . . . and will therefore concentrate its efforts on this ideal: to eventually provide every individual in the United States with equal opportunity of access to that part of the total information resource which will satisfy the individual's educational, working, cultural, and leisure time needs and interests, regardless of the individual's location, social or physical condition or level of intellectual achievement."

To make progress toward this goal, the commission determined to "strengthen, develop or create where needed, human and material resources which are supportive of high quality library and information services; and join together the library and information facilities in the country through a common pattern of organization, uniform standards, and shared communications, to form a nationwide network."

The proposed and recommended national program of the NCLIS "represents an overall structure . . . a framework for planned systematic growth of library and information services . . ."

> 1. Ensure that basic minimums of library and information services adequate to meet the needs of all local communities are satisfied.

There is here an implicit commitment for the NCLIS to support categorical aid under LSCA, ESEA and HEA, and the Medical Library Act of 1974, and the NCLIS goes on record as working for a revised and expanded LSCA in 1976.

> 2. Provide adequate special services to special constituencies, including the unserved.

These include the large user constituencies which require materials and services of a highly specialized nature. Such groups include, specifically, the poor, the illiterate, the blind, the visually and physically handicapped, the ethnic minorities, American Indians on reservations, the very young, senior citizens, inner-city youths, migrant workers, the institutionalized, and many others. The large number belonging to ethnic minorities—40 million Black, Asian and Hispanic Americans—and the special barriers to access of American Indians (and the special treaty responsibilities of the federal government toward them) are mentioned.

3. Strengthen existing statewide resources and systems.

It is emphasized that the states are essential building blocks in any national information system, and that "any new national program should rest on the understanding that the federal government would fund those aspects of the National Program that are of common concern nationally, in return for a commitment on the part of the states to accept, in cooperation with the local governments, a fair share of the responsibility for funding libraries within their own jurisdictions.

4. Ensure basic and continuing education of personnel essential to the implementation of a National Program.

A federally funded program of fellowships and training institutes is basic, the recommendation notes state, to the fulfillment of this responsibility.

5. Coordinate existing Federal programs of library and information service.

Since the National Program will make use of the national services of the Library of Congress, the National Library of Medicine and the National Agricultural Library it must ensure that they are able to continue at levels strong enough to fully satisfy the national need.

6. Encourage the private sector (comprising organizations which are not directly tax supported) to become an active partner in the development of the National Program.

Special libraries and information centers and services (in both for-profit and not-for-profit organizations) and various service organizations, must be tied in to any viable and complete information system.

7. Establish a locus of Federal responsibility charged with implementing the national network and coordinating the National Program under the policy guidance of the Commission.

The point is made that the NCLIS is not empowered by law to operate programs, but as a matter of first priority some agency in the federal establishment must become the locus of federal responsibility for libraries—where policy can be translated into action . . . It would have authority to make grants and contracts, establish standards, and encourage their adoption, and undertake further functions consistent with commission policy.

It might not be necessary to create a new agency—proposed functions might be assigned to several agencies . . . but there would have to be new administrative and operational functions for which at present there seems to be no natural home.

The NCLIS goes firmly on record as saying that "the responsibility of the agency, whether old or new, should neither be all-encompassing, nor authoritarian, nor prescriptive, nor regulatory, but rather supportive and coordinating. It would have no control whatsoever over the content of the information flowing over the nationwide network.

"It would, however, be backed by legislation to enable it to obtain the necessary funding from the Congress for meeting the crucial needs of the National Program. It would be authorized to require compliance with standards for nationwide compatibility as a condition of continued funding.

"Whatever central authority is eventually established to direct the National Program, local autonomy and the maximum degree possible of local self-determination should be one of the program's major tenets. The variations of needs and the existing levels of services and resources are so great that it would be difficult for a central authority to be fully cognizant of the diverse needs of all."

It is not yet clear, the NCLIS report states, where an agency responsible for library and information service belongs in the organizational hierarchy of the federal government, or whether there is an existing agency to which this role would be appropriate. Three existing agencies have been mentioned as possibilities:

1. The Library of Congress
2. The Office of Libraries and Learning Resources, U. S. Office of Education
3. The National Commission on Libraries and Information Science

8. Plan, develop and implement a nation-wide network of library and information service.

To bring about all this will require new legislation which would need to define the total program; assign responsibilities and functions; provide needed authorizations; specify criteria for participation in the network; and authorize multi-year appropriations commensurate with program and accountability requirements.

The commission's goals go into some detail about the network concept:

"A nationwide network of libraries and information centers means an integrated system encompassing state networks, multi-state networks, and specialized networks . . . the Federal government would force no library or information service to join the network, but it would provide technical inducements and funding incentives to state government and the private sector to strengthen their ability to affiliate." Bibliographic and technical standardization—such as that already developed by the Library of Congress, would produce further economies of scale and reduce needless duplication and incompatibility of information that could lead to stoppage of the free flow through the network.

The possibility of making unique resource collections available nation-wide is an exhilarating one, but the responsible operating agency would need to provide funds to enable public or private institutions to protect their collections and serve those outside their primary clientele. The collection of the Glass Information Center in Corning, New York, or Chemical Abstracts service in Columbus, Ohio, are but two examples of the information riches stored in private collections that could be made widely available.

The NCLIS has published a document into which it has had many inputs from librarians and others most closely concerned; now the task is to elicit even wider discussion and suggestions as to ways and means of implementation and evolution of the National Program Plan.

One proposed means of doing this would be the White House Conference on Libraries and Information Service which a Joint Resolution of Congress authorized and requested the President to call not later than 1978. Public Law 93-568 states that "The purpose of the White House Conference on Libraries and Information Services . . . shall be to develop recommendations for the further improvement of the Nation's libraries and information centers, and their use by the public."

The NCLIS was authorized to make technical and financial assistance available to the states and territories to enable them to organize and conduct state conferences in preparation for the National Conference. Many members of Congress felt, in authorizing the conference, that the state and regional meetings to examine, recommend and plan local, state-wide, and federal responsibilities and relationships would be the most vital part of the undertaking.

"These state meetings will be designed to insure that the recommendations of the public become a central concern of the White House Conference. Two thirds of those attending each state conference, therefore, will be citizens not associated with libraries, and one third of those attending will be from the professional library and information community. The state conferences will force each of the states to evaluate its own library programs and to engage in systematic statewide planning in order to be able to bring to the White House Conference coherent suggestions with respect to the Federal role in financing library and information services." Thus, John Brademas, member of Congress from Indiana.

There is authorization, but as yet no appropriation, for up to $3.5 million to carry out the White House Conference and to assist the states with their own conferences. NCLIS will administer the project, and an appropriation and a call from the President for conference planning to get under way were pending when this was being written.

Meanwhile, many ideas about money—how to finance the complex and essential library and information enterprise—were being suggested.

Members of the NCLIS voted unanimously to place a statement on the record, and before the public, concerning the continuing need for federal funds that are specifically designated to develop and sustain library and information programs, and the poor substitute that revenue sharing has shown itself to be for the great majority of libraries:

"In its effort to work toward improved library and information programs, the NCLIS has closely monitored changing library funding patterns, including revenue sharing. Recent reports including studies of the U. S. Department of Treasury and other governmental organizations and professional associations indicate that libraries are last in funding among the eight priority areas eligible for general revenue sharing. Though individual libraries have benefited from revenue sharing, the overall funding pattern has provided only a small fraction of the amounts available in earlier years from categorical funds."

According to *Alternatives for Financing the Public Library,* a study prepared for the NCLIS and published in May of 1974, an "actual use" report issued in March of that year and covering the first three entitlement, payments under revenue sharing yielded only $18 million for primarily public libraries. This total represents only *one* per cent of the $1.8 billion in revenue sharing funds actually expended by local governments during the first half of 1973. The percentage expended for libraries has not gone up much in the intervening months if at all. Figures from Arizona, for instance, might be considered high: fourteen communities received a total of $584,832 in 1973, almost all of it for capital outlays.

The *Alternatives* study examined options available to the status quo, and recommended the following:

a) increased federal support to meet upgraded library services and development needs

b) revised LSCA to reflect strengthened federal role and mandate coordinated federal-state planning for a national program of library services

c) increased state support to reflect prime responsibility for public library maintenance and support

d) decreased local support role

e) staged approach over a ten-year period to achieve balance in intergovernmental funding pattern ending with:

> Federal—20%
> State—50%
> Local—30%

of a progressively elevated national expenditure for improved and expanded public library services

By the mid '70s, talk of "fee or free" filled the air—how much information and in what depth should be provided— not really free but by public monies, to all? What should the role of commercial information services be? How could special libraries of companies who paid well to develop competitive information for their own use be tied in to a network through which the information could be accessible to all? Does federal money that must be matched by the state or locality discriminate against the very libraries and people who need it most? These and other questions buzzed around the heads of commission members, library leaders, and thoughtful citizens, like angry hornets.

And in the meantime, with every day that passed, the tide of need for information rises, and the tide of information increases, while the gulf between needer and supply widens because tragically, the would-be user not only cannot get at what he needs, but often does not even know that what he needs exists. All the plans, the legislation and the networks are ultimately for users—actual, would be, or might be.

Library professionals have been trying for decades to find out more about the people who actually do now use libraries. The "actual user" profile has remained remarkably constant for the past thirty years or more: White, middle-class, likely to be female, young, and perhaps a student, urban or suburban, and educated beyond the high school level. When the National Advisory Commission on Libraries did its information gathering (1966–67) users were defined as adults who claimed to have visited a library at least once during the preceding month period at the time they were interviewed. By this criterion, three out of every ten adults in the United States were characterized as library users, using mostly public libraries. Libraries other than public (academic, professional, special) were used by only a minute proportion of the total user-adult population, about 13 per cent of them. Of these adults, 5 per cent were classified as light users; 3 per cent as moderate users; and 5 per cent as heavy users. All library use seems to decline with age, and among people of fifty years or more, only two out of ten ever visit a library.

Findings as to reasons given for use are especially interesting. The three most frequently given were: 1) to get information on special problems; 2) to borrow non-fiction books; and 3) to borrow fiction books. Each of the three reasons was given by about half of those queried. It is apparent that the information function of the library has become at least as important as the "creative reading" function, or developmental long-range functions, since "to use reference books and periodicals" was cited almost as often as the first three. "Add to this," said the report, "the 35% who report that they use libraries in order to aid their children with homework, the 15% who wish to examine documents, and the 10% who attend lectures, exhibits or performances, and we readily see that contemporary libraries are no longer mere circulation sources."

Beginning in about 1966, explorations of the needs of non-users began in real earnest: the aged, the rural and urban poor, the minority-ethnic groups, the culturally different or isolated from the mainstream by language, location, culture, and the rest—all of the groups which both the ALA professional objectives and the NCLIS goals now pledge themselves to try to reach and serve. Various investigators have pointed out that lack of adult use of libraries is characteristic of poverty areas, which are likely also to be areas of high concentration of low educational attainment, low self-esteem, socially disorganized and culturally disoriented people. It has been emphasized too, that the very concepts upon which library use is predicated are middle class in their supposition of stability, privacy, routine, and belief in self and the future.

Yet despite all of this, the outreach efforts of libraries have shown that people living in even the most despairing community can be taught to bring their survival needs to those libraries which are committed to providing a response. Further, the scattered and sometimes unsustained efforts have proven that there are as many potential dreamers, creators, lovers of art and poetry, in poor neighborhoods as there are in middle-class ones, and that libraries can provide for the emotional, often unarticulated, needs as well as the "crisis" ones.

There is evidence, furthermore, that the potential users learn quickly with exposure to value libraries for their developmental uses as much as for their "coping" help with jobs, housing, or health.

A recent (1972) study of primarily rural people in southwestern Louisiana found that "many non-users lack confidence to engage in what they consider to be difficult intellectual pursuits." It was observed that non-users had less self-confidence, less self-esteem and could not, or believed they could not, read or do other things as well as others. Often they saw no need to. For many non-users perceive learning—and by extension, libraries and library use—as something they were finished with when they left school. By contrast, library users in this same study were involved people who translated stimuli from many areas of life and activity into a need for library use.

One is struck by the not unexpected fact that the needs of each of the subgroups identified as requiring special attention are in fact the needs of all groups within the society, intensified in one particular or another. Primarily, above all else the needs spell out a more knowledgeable, interested, available, inventive, creative, eclectic library staff. Specialized materials, yes; better delivery systems, of course: but the key is the people who make library service in every instance.

It is very evident, too, that the special needs of particular groups must be considered and programmed in a context of, and as a genuine part of, total, regular service patterns. These user-oriented programs for the yet-to-be-reached users must have specific commitment in terms of planning and the setting of objectives, but they must not be seen as add-ons, apart from the "real work" of the library, the system or the network. The over-all implication is that there is, and must be, in the making a whole new way of conducting *all* library services for *all* user groups—those who constitute special challenges and those who do not.

What, after all, are the hallmarks of quality library service, and are they not exactly what has been called for, with particular adaptations, by all of the special-attention groups identified?

1. Humaneness, acceptance, respect, concern for all users in dealings that all library workers —professional and otherwise—have with them;

2. Library staff members who are prepared and knowledgeable in terms of individual differences as to language, educational level, and needs and are able to tailor and personalize their assistance;

3. Willingness and ability to take programs and services to people where they are and where they need them, in every sense: physically and psychologically;

4. Materials and equipment in all formats that are geared to the handicaps, sensibilities, interests and abilities of those who want to use them;

5. More deliberate and integrated use of nonprint with print materials so that there is continuous, conscious building of use-links between them;

6. Involvement of users in developing policies and programs so that there is a real sense of community control and participation in planning and achieving individual and "corporate" goals through the library;

7. Much fuller, ordered, utilization of paraprofessionals, as communicators on a two-way channel between the library and its users, as coordinators with other agencies, and as instruments of one-to-one user services. Of special importance is the involvement of individuals from hard-to-reach or hard-to-service groups.

Fragmentations and categorization of special groups would fade once tailored, careful, expert service becomes the objective for all users!

Finally, how is it all going to be made to happen? We have goals, we have objectives; we have the outline of a structure, and action steps for going ahead; and most of all we have users and would-be users, and could-be users ready and waiting. The reality of all the numbers, all the statistics is that they are not abstractions but people. Once they have been translated in the mind's eye from numbers into *persons,* they can never quite be translated back again and dealt with in terms of national interest, economic gain, threats to peace, community guilt, self-interest, or even sympathy. Even political expediency is not likely to work any better as a determinant of what users to serve, or serve better, first.

Setting priorities, as librarians have been finding out, is most difficult and unpopular work, for it means invariably that some segment comes in for more attention—and more funds—than others, at least for some period of time. Acceptance of priorities in the common interest can be achieved—as witness the relative cheerfulness with which childless citizens pay huge taxes for support of the public schools. It will take a "jog" to get on course, and superior leadership to make the priorities stick but that is what the ALA, the NCLIS, and the Congress are, I take it, all about.

John W. Gardner, one of America's most creative thinkers and movers—the founder and director of Common Cause—has this to say:

"An important thing to understand about any institution or social system is that it doesn't move unless it is pushed. And what is generally needed is not a mild push but a solid jolt. If the push is not administered by vigorous and purposeful leaders, it will be administered eventually by an aroused citizenry or by a crisis."

How to administer the jolt and get results? Here are some thoughts that occur to this library advocate about implementation of the National Plan—which would also be in line as well, thankfully, with the ALA goals and objectives and the recommendations of the Martin study and others. And that indeed is something to be thankful for:

basically, the profession, the commission, the Congress and friends and users of libraries and information services see eye to eye on what should be done; the tough part now is how to start getting it done.

First, I believe that the public policy concerning libraries and their vital importance to all the people of the United States should be communicated—at saturation level —to the American people; that the NCLIS, coalescing all the forces at its command should project the library not as a place but as a function; the librarians as professionals who carry with them wherever they go their ability to listen, to diagnose to prescribe—like doctors, rather than like pharmacists who must stand behind their rows of pills and bottles simply to supply exactly what has been asked for.

Second, the NCLIS should in my opinion—perhaps jointly with the ALA—and as an essential foundation to network building, outline a User Services Expectations policy, including a set of user-satisfaction goals at several levels; again this should be widely disseminated to explain how the network concept with the accompanying standardization and library linkages helps to make it possible.

Third, it is essential, in my opinion, that the responsible operating agency for the program plan provide a framework and some methodologies, some instruments and criteria for assessing user priorities locally, setting objectives, and measuring progress toward achievement of those objectives. This could be subcontracted to ALA for working out.

Fourth, models of local library linkage—grass-roots networking—should be provided for either under Title III (interlibrary co-operation) of an expanded LSCA or preferably under a new piece of cross-type-of-library act (Library and Information Network Development Act, perhaps) which would be understood to relate to all types of libraries. To be most successful I believe that initial grass-roots networking experiences should be targeted at particular client groups. For example, the State Library Agency (which should administer such grants) would fund a public library system and several community colleges to develop integrated service to students; or a school system and public library system for joint and integrated services to preschool children in the community.

Fifth, while the National Program is being implemented and the network and new funding patterns are being established from the local community up, we need, I believe, to have help and encouragement given to libraries to seek and utilize funds from existing federal and state programs. There are already some examples of libraries that are doing this, but many more could be helped to. For example, there is the Department of Housing and Urban Development's block grant, the Housing and Community Development Act—Title I; regulations, revised, thanks in large part to ALA's Washington efforts now makes libraries eligible (neighborhood branch facilities). Shortly after the regulations were revised, the public library in Johnson City, Tennessee, got $100,000 to buy a library site after gaining approval from city agencies.

The Comprehensive Employment and Training Act funding, through the Department of Labor, can provide training and important community information services at the same time, if libraries learn to utilize it. The Los Angeles Public Library has opened a Community Information and Referral Service—a telephone and walk-in service staffed with librarian, part-time workers from library schools and three clerical workers—a total of thirteen; all are paid from CETA funds.

With funding from the Illinois Arts Council, the Illinois State Library has launched a program to give greater visibility to Illinois writers and their work. A total of thirty-six public libraries will participate in the Writers-to-the-People Project, with author visits, lectures, readings, and discussion groups.

A list of state and federally funded programs with which libraries of all kinds might collaborate should be a basic tool for consultants and technical assistants who will work out of the National Program operating agency, as well as State Library staff.

The NCLIS, ALA and other leadership should also

work for widespread acceptance of the proposition that funds for Intensive Care or Super Services—extensive adaptations of generally good general-user services—should be built into the budgets of other agencies, organizations, institutions, and programs that also serve these extra requirement groups (drug addicts, aged, probationers) such as police departments, day care centers, nursing homes, or health agencies. This would give such other agencies and members of the private sector a real involvement—a "piece of the action" in fact, in development of the library and information networks.

For a sixth point, it is important, I believe, that money be built into the National Program authorization for research—and not just research on the network itself, geared to technology and standardization for example, but research also on motivation and facilitation of *use* of the library and information network. For example, the idea of strengthening of libraries to undertake the production of materials—materials oriented narrowly to the needs of a specific community or subgroup, such as oral history on tapes, or cassettes (video) for home use on TV. There should be surveys, too, for instance of the ways in which libraries and museums now co-ordinate programs, and ways in which they could do more.

Finally, and this is perhaps the most important point of all: since networks made up of weak grass-roots links will be meaningless—a sharing of inadequacies—I would suggest that no type of library or library system be eligible for inclusion in the network until it has reached a minimum per capita expenditure. Based on the fact that at present the best-served communities in the country now benefit from the services of public, school, and post-secondary institution libraries each one of which spends more than ten dollars per capita (the public library based on the total population, the education agencies based on their own student populations), I believe this requirement is basic if the network is to have meaning and strength, and that each type of library or library system should join the network with its own ten-dollars per capita minimum. In addition then, any libraries (or local library systems) of different types (public, school, and community college, or public, research, and college) belonging to the network which serve all or part of the same population in a community or region *should share in a special additional grant of ten dollars for every student of any age and at every level who spends at least two hours or more a day in structured learning or research*—to make the network work at the community level.

All of these proposals are only words until they become action. Libraries stand poised to do a job that no other agency, or agencies, are prepared to do. They may not know yet exactly how they are going to do it, but they know for sure that library and information services are an idea whose time has come.

Since man first collected, passed on, and remembered his experience, some member of the community was made responsible for enlarging and using the precious body of knowledge. Librarianship is both old and new, but its expectations are unlimited.

APPENDIX

Appendix I:

FEDERAL ALLOTMENT UNDER THE LIBRARY SERVICES AND CONSTRUCTION ACT
P.L. 84-597, as Amended by P.L. 91-600
Title I, Library Services

Fiscal Year 1975 [1]*State Allotments and Matching Requirements*

States and Outlying Areas	Federal Allotment	State and Local Matching	Federal Percentage	State Percentage
TOTALS	49,155,000	49,557,860	–	–
Alabama	843,067	486,063	63.43	36.57
Alaska	259,845	358,833	42.00	58.00
Arizona	575,938	490,417	54.01	45.99
Arkansas	569,047	323,996	63.72	36.28
California	3,945,238	5,097,251	43.63	56.37
Colorado	647,572	615,983	51.25	48.75
Connecticut	758,558	1,191,964	38.89	61.11
Delaware	303,914	388,057	43.92	56.08
District of Columbia	333,111	676,317	33.00	67.00
Florida	1,604,555	1,399,105	53.42	46.58
Georgia	1,073,744	804,744	57.16	42.84
Hawaii	352,515	462,926	43.23	56.77
Idaho	340,728	238,348	58.84	41.16
Illinois	2,226,767	2,999,158	42.61	57.39
Indiana	1,161,880	1,110,524	51.13	48.87
Iowa	719,205	645,511	52.70	47.30
Kansas	610,576	605,710	50.20	49.80
Kentucky	803,533	521,554	60.64	39.36
Louisiana	879,337	559,134	61.13	38.87
Maine	388,423	267,808	59.19	40.81
Maryland	938,820	1,113,694	45.74	54.26
Massachusetts	1,251,648	1,526,705	45.05	54.95
Michigan	1,843,212	2,126,661	46.43	53.57
Minnesota	905,451	858,186	51.34	48.66
Mississippi	620,188	319,490	66.00	34.00

States and Outlying Areas	Federal Allotment	State and Local Matching	Percentages	
			Federal Percentage	State Percentage
Missouri	1,064,676	950,992	52.82	47.18
Montana	332,385	254,971	56.59	43.41
Nebraska	478,009	448,186	51.61	48.39
Nevada	299,924	410,965	42.19	57.81
New Hampshire	343,992	292,087	54.08	45.92
New Jersey	1,528,388	2,108,034	42.03	57.97
New Mexico	399,304	259,939	60.57	39.43
New York	3,503,108	5,298,671	39.80	60.20
North Carolina	1,161,517	801,168	59.18	40.82
North Dakota	315,157	216,664	59.26	40.74
Ohio	2,148,242	2,216,329	49.22	50.78
Oklahoma	684,023	497,773	57.88	42.12
Oregon	602,415	544,824	52.51	47.49
Pennsylvania	2,351,173	2,343,661	50.08	49.92
Rhode Island	375,365	372,374	50.20	49.80
South Carolina	693,997	412,327	62.73	37.27
South Dakota	323,681	221,696	59.35	40.65
Tennessee	942,628	608,768	60.76	39.24
Texas	2,345,007	1,920,193	54.98	45.02
Utah	408,552	282,270	59.14	40.86
Vermont	284,509	222,276	65.14	43.86
Virginia	1,078,459	926,111	53.80	46.20
Washington	822,212	856,799	48.97	51.03
West Virginia	524,254	326,117	61.65	38.35
Wisconsin	1,023,147	912,065	52.87	47.13
Wyoming	264,017	229,934	53.45	46.55
American Samoa	44,925	23,143	66.00	34.00
Trust Territory	56,492	-0-	100.00	-0-
Guam	55,414	28,547	66.00	34.00
Puerto Rico	691,827	356,395	66.00	34.00
Virgin Islands	51,329	26,442	66.00	34.00

1/ Estimated distribution of $49,155,000 with a basic amount of $200,000 to the 50 States, D.C. and Puerto Rico, $40,000 to the other outlying areas, and the balance distributed on the total resident population, 7/1/73, 4/1/70 for the areas. Required matching amounts are computed on FY 1974075 "Federal Share" percentages.

Appendix II:

FEDERAL ALLOTMENT UNDER THE LIBRARY SERVICES AND CONSTRUCTION ACT

P.L. 84-597, as Amended by P.L. 91-600
Title III, Interlibrary Cooperation, Revised for FY 1975[1]

LSCA Title III	Federal Allotment	LSCA Title III	Federal Allotment
Total	$2,594,000		
Alabama	47,898	New Jersey	56,314
Alaska	40,736	New Mexico	42,448
Arizona	44,617	New York	80,567
Arkansas	44,532	North Carolina	51,809
California	85,997	North Dakota	41,414
Colorado	45,497	Ohio	63,927
Connecticut	46,860	Oklahoma	45,944
Delaware	41,276	Oregon	44,942
District of Columbia	41,635	Pennsylvania	66,419
Florida	57,250	Rhode Island	42,154
Georgia	50,731	South Carolina	46,067
Hawaii	41,873	South Dakota	41,519
Idaho	41,728	Tennessee	49,121
Illinois	64,892	Texas	66,344
Indiana	51,813	Utah	42,561
Iowa	46,377	Vermont	41,038
Kansas	45,042	Virginia	50,789
Kentucky	47,412	Washington	47,642
Louisiana	48,343	West Virginia	43,982
Maine	42,314	Wisconsin	50,109
Maryland	49,074	Wyoming	40,787
Massachusetts	52,916	American Samoa	10,060
Michigan	60,181	Trust Territory	10,203
Minnesota	48,664	Guam	10,189
Mississippi	45,160	Puerto Rico	46,040
Missouri	50,619	Virgin Islands	10,139
Montana	41,626		
Nebraska	43,414		
Nevada	41,227		
New Hampshire	41,768		

[1] Distribution of $2,594,000 with a minimum allotment of $40,000 to the 50 States, D.C., and Puerto Rico; $10,000 for the other outlying areas, and the balance distributed on the basis of the total resident population, 7/1/73 for the 50 States and D.C. and 4/1/70 for the outlying areas.

Appendix III:

Libraries and Instructional Resources (ESEA IV B) (Consolidation Program)

	(For 1976) 1975 Appropriation	1976 Budget Request	1976 House Allowance	1976 Senate Allowance	Conference Agreement
TOTALS	$137,330,000	$137,330,000	$147,330,000	$147,330,000	$147,330,000
Alabama	2,339,205	2,340,573	2,510,756	2,510,756	2,510,756
Alaska	250,818	246,786	264,730	264,730	264,730
Arizona	1,424,113	1,382,003	1,482,488	1,482,488	1,482,488
Arkansas	1,301,669	1,288,484	1,382,170	1,382,170	1,382,170
California	12,556,971	12,697,802	13,621,059	13,621,059	13,621,059
Colorado	1,608,365	1,600,214	1,716,565	1,716,565	1,716,565
Connecticut	1,949,787	1,956,106	2,098,334	2,098,334	2,098,334
Delaware	396,667	381,069	409,635	409,635	409,635
Florida	4,403,497	4,455,141	4,779,074	4,779,074	4,779,074
Georgia	3,144,880	3,179,646	3,410,838	3,410,838	3,410,838
Hawaii	547,061	545,527	585,193	585,193	585,193
Idaho	543,278	524,745	562,900	562,900	562,900
Illinois	7,112,491	7,149,007	7,668,812	7,668,812	7,668,812
Indiana	3,485,011	3,480,985	3,734,087	3,734,087	3,734,087
Iowa	1,863,613	1,859,989	1,995,229	1,995,229	1,995,229

Kansas	1,365,042	1,392,394	1,493,635	1,493,635	1,493,635
Kentucky	2,140,299	2,145,741	2,301,758	2,301,758	2,301,758
Louisiana	2,686,649	2,647,107	2,839,578	2,839,578	2,839,578
Maine	707,173	675,415	724,524	724,524	724,524
Maryland	2,676,362	2,693,867	2,889,738	2,889,738	2,889,738
Massachusetts	3,606,859	3,613,470	3,876,205	3,876,205	3,876,205
Michigan	6,186,270	6,143,678	6,590,385	6,590,385	6,590,385
Minnesota	2,659,822	2,634,118	2,825,645	2,825,645	2,825,645
Mississippi	1,642,403	1,615,800	1,733,285	1,733,285	1,733,285
Missouri	2,973,213	2,971,826	3,187,907	3,187,907	3,187,907
Montana	512,205	498,768	535,033	535,033	535,033
Nebraska	986,873	981,949	1,053,347	1,053,347	1,053,347
Nevada	369,743	358,489	384,555	384,555	384,555
New Hampshire	532,849	514,354	551,753	551,753	551,753
New Jersey	4,521,454	4,623,995	4,960,205	4,960,205	4,960,205
New Mexico	828,198	802,705	861,069	861,069	861,069
New York	10,823,688	11,004,068	11,804,175	11,804,175	11,804,175
North Carolina	3,345,702	3,364,086	3,608,689	3,608,689	3,608,689
North Dakota	436,953	433,824	465,368	465,368	465,368
Ohio	7,044,168	6,977,556	7,484,894	7,484,894	7,484,894
Oklahoma	1,642,470	1,618,398	1,736,072	1,736,072	1,736,072
Oregon	1,360,213	1,363,819	1,462,982	1,462,982	1,462,982

	(For 1976) 1975 Appropriation	1976 Budget Request	1976 House Allowance	1976 Senate Allowance	Conference Agreement
Pennsylvania	7,313,595	7,258,113	7,785,850	7,785,850	7,785,850
Rhode Island	591,999	581,898	624,206	624,206	624,206
South Carolina	1,849,041	1,836,609	1,970,149	1,970,149	1,970,149
South Dakota	475,743	459,802	493,234	493,234	493,234
Tennessee	2,572,743	2,561,381	2,747,619	2,747,619	2,747,619
Texas	7,801,883	7,710,121	8,270,725	8,270,725	8,270,725
Utah	843,256	813,096	872,216	872,216	872,216
Vermont	326,157	303,937	326,036	326,036	326,036
Virginia	3,081,125	3,091,322	3,316,092	3,316,092	3,316,092
Washington	2,179,843	2,174,317	2,332,411	2,332,411	2,332,411
West Virginia	1,129,343	1,096,250	1,175,959	1,175,959	1,175,959
Wisconsin	3,090,423	3,060,149	3,282,653	3,282,653	3,282,653
Wyoming	247,648	231,200	248,010	248,010	248,010
District of Columbia	410,468	402,651	431,928	431,928	431,928
Puerto Rico	(3,430,699)	(3,584,852)	2,386,940	2,386,940	2,386,940
Outlying Areas			1,473,852	1,473,300	1,473,300

1/ This does not reflect the "hold harmless" provision.

Appendix IV:

Undergraduate Instructional Equipment Library Resources (HEA VI)

	1975 Appropriation	1976 Budget Request	1976 House Allowance	1976 Senate Allowance	Conference Agreement
TOTALS	$7,500,000	—	—	$15,000,000	$7,500,00
Alabama	119,066	—	—	244,223	122,111
Alaska	7,435	—	—	13,915	6,958
Arizona	99,431	—	—	219,942	109,971
Arkansas	53,138	—	—	104,002	52,001
California	938,918	—	—	1,889,133	944,565
Colorado	107,961	—	—	220,985	110,493
Connecticut	93,795	—	—	188,249	94,124
Delaware	20,502	—	—	41,309	20,655
Florida	220,155	—	—	444,668	222,335
Georgia	134,284	—	—	260,902	130,452
Hawaii	33,140	—	—	63,176	31,588
Idaho	31,401	—	—	61,425	30,713
Illinois	347,970	—	—	693,475	346,738
Indiana	167,429	—	—	319,977	159,989
Iowa	101,829	—	—	198,011	99,005

	1975 Appropriation	1976 Budget Request	1976 House Allowance	1976 Senate Allowance	Conference Agreement
Kansas	90,704	—	—	175,574	87,787
Kentucky	98,604	—	—	194,369	97,184
Louisiana	128,475	—	—	250,763	125,381
Maine	34,379	—	—	64,878	32,439
Maryland	124,279	—	—	244,413	122,206
Massachusetts	259,976	—	—	528,345	264,173
Michigan	303,539	—	—	608,279	304,140
Minnesota	137,236	—	—	266,270	133,135
Mississippi	84,389	—	—	165,331	82,666
Missouri	161,054	—	—	307,593	153,796
Montana	25,617	—	—	50,984	25,492
Nebraska	56,639	—	—	106,087	53,044
Nevada	14,864	—	—	35,095	17,548
New Hampshire	30,771	—	—	62,184	31,092
New Jersey	169,609	—	—	349,228	174,614
New Mexico	42,983	—	—	86,060	43,030
New York	609,258	—	—	1,267,499	633,749
North Carolina	193,007	—	—	391,400	195,700
North Dakota	28,747	—	—	50,660	25,330
Ohio	320,120	—	—	629,752	314,876

Oklahoma	109,025	—	—	215,863	107,931
Oregon	105,569	—	—	205,179	102,590
Pennsylvania	353,356	—	—	694,385	347,192
Rhode Island	41,984	—	—	85,173	42,586
South Carolina	93,794	—	—	198,958	99,479
South Dakota	25,184	—	—	49,171	24,586
Tennessee	143,448	—	—	284,130	142,065
Texas	432,534	—	—	863,731	431,865
Utah	76,255	—	—	147,512	73,756
Vermont	26,194	—	—	51,587	25,794
Virginia	152,182	—	—	313,628	156,814
Washington	156,367	—	—	307,657	153,829
West Virginia	61,914	—	—	119,503	59,751
Wisconsin	180,070	—	—	356,110	178,055
Wyoming	13,338	—	—	27,645	13,822
District of Columbia	50,276	—	—	99,935	49,967
American Samoa	674	—	—	1,149	575
Guam	3,018	—	—	5,942	2,971
Puerto Rico	82,814	—	—	172,013	86,006
Trust Territory	58	—	—	300	150
Virgin Islands	1,242	—	—	2,273	1,136

Appendix V:

GUIDE TO OE-ADMINISTERED PROGRAMS, FISCAL YEAR 1975

GROUP I: TO INSTITUTIONS, AGENCIES, AND ORGANIZATION
PART A—For Elementary and Secondary Education Programs

TYPE OF ASSISTANCE	AUTHORIZING LEGISLATION	PURPOSE	APPRO-PRIATION (dollars)	WHO MAY APPLY	WHERE TO APPLY
1 Bilingual education (OMB Cat. No. 13.402)[1]	Elementary and Secondary Education Act, Title VII	To develop and operate programs for children ages 3-18 who have limited English-speaking ability, to train bilingual education personnel, to improve bilingual education, to develop curriculum materials	85,000,000	Local education agencies or institutions of higher education applying jointly with local education agencies, institutions of higher education, and individuals	OE Grant Application Control Center
2 Comprehensive planning and evaluation (OMB Cat. No. 13.542)	Elementary and Secondary Education Act, Title V-C	To improve State and local comprehensive planning and evaluation of education programs	4,750,000	State and local education agencies	OE Division of State Assistance
3 Follow Through (OMB Cat. No. 13.433)	Community Services Act (P.L. 93-644), Title V	To extend into primary grades the educational gains made by deprived children in Head Start or similar preschool programs	53,000,000	Local education or other agencies nominated by State education agencies in accordance with OE criteria	OE Grant Application Control Center
4 Incentive grants (OMB Cat. No. 13.512)	Elementary and Secondary Education Act, Title I, Part B	To encourage greater State and local expenditures for education	14,000,000	State education agencies that exceed the national effort index	OE Division of Education for the Disadvantaged

5 Innovative and exemplary programs—supplementary centers (OMB Cat. No. 13.516 and 13.519)	Elementary and Secondary Education Act, Title III	To support innovative and exemplary projects	120,000,000[2]	Local education agencies	State education agencies or OE Grant Application Control Center
6 Indian education (OMB Cat. No. 13.534)	Indian Education Act (P.L. 92-318), Title IV, Part A	To provide financial assistance to local education agencies on a formula basis for supplemental programs designed to meet the special educational needs of Indian students enrolled in public schools	25,000,000[3]	Local education agencies and Indian controlled schools on or near reservations	OE Office of Indian Education
7 Indian education (OMB Cat. No. 13.535)	Indian Education Act (P.L. 92-318), Title IV, Part B	To extend the development of exemplary activities which provide special programs to improve educational opportunities for Indian children	12,000,000	Indian tribes, organizations and institutions; State and local education agencies, and federally supported elementary and secondary schools for Indian children	OE Office of Indian Education
8 Programs for children in State institutions for the neglected and delinquent (OMB Cat. No. 13.431)	Elementary and Secondary Education Act, Title I	To improve the education of delinquent and neglected children in State institutions	26,820,749	Eligible State agencies	State education agencies
9 Programs for disadvantaged children (OMB Cat. No. 13.428)	Elementary and Secondary Education Act, Title I	To meet the educational needs of deprived children	1,569,563,964	Local school districts	State education agencies
10 Programs for Indian children (OMB Cat. No. 13.428)	Elementary and Secondary Education Act, Title I	To provide additional educational assistance to Indian children in federally operated schools	11,567,233	Bureau of Indian Affairs schools	Bureau of Indian Affairs, Department of Interior

TYPE OF ASSISTANCE	AUTHORIZING LEGISLATION	PURPOSE	APPRO-PRIATION (dollars)	WHO MAY APPLY	WHERE TO APPLY
11 Programs for migratory children (OMB Cat. No. 13.429)	Elementary and Secondary Education	To meet the educational needs of children of migratory farm workers	91,953,160	Local school districts	State education agencies
12 School library resources and instructional materials (OMB Cat. No. 13.480)	Elementary and Secondary Education Act, Title II	To help provide school library resources, textbooks, and other instructional materials	95,250,000	Local education agencies	OE Office of Libraries and Learning Resources
13 Special grants to urban and rural school districts with high concentrations of poor children (OMB Cat. No. 13.511)	Elementary and Secondary Education Act, Title I, Part C	To improve the education of disadvantaged children	38,000,000	Local school districts	State education agencies
14 State administration of ESEA Title I programs (OMB Cat. No. 13.430)	Elementary and Secondary Education Act, Title I	To strengthen administration of ESEA, Title I	19,315,021	State education agencies	OE Division of Education for the Disadvantaged
15 Strengthening State education agencies (OMB Cat. No. 13.485 and 13.486)	Elementary and Secondary Education Act, Title V-A	To improve leadership resources of State education agencies	34,675,000	State education agencies, combinations thereof, and public regional interstate commissions	OE Division of State Assistance or OE Grant Application Control Center
16 Right to Read (OMB Cat. No. 13.533)	Cooperative Research Act (P.L. 83-531)	To provide facilitating services and resources to stimulate institutions, governmental agencies, and private organizations to improve and expand reading related activities	12,000,000	State and local education agencies, institutions of higher education, and other public and private nonprofit agencies	OE Grant Application Control Center

	Authority	Purpose	Amount	Recipient	OE Office
17 School health and nutrition services (OMB Cat. No. 13.523)	Elementary and Secondary Education Act, Title IV	To support demonstration projects designed to improve nutrition and health services in public and private schools serving areas with high concentrations of children from low-income families	900,000	Local education agencies (exceptional cases, private nonprofit educational organizations)	OE Grant Application Control Center
18 School maintenance and operation (OMB Cat. No. 13.478)	School Assistance in Federally Affected Areas (P.L. 81-874)	To aid school districts on which Federal activities or major disasters have placed a financial burden	636,016,000	Local school districts	OE Division of School Assistance in Federally Affected Areas
19 Education and the Arts (OMB Cat. No. 13.566)	Education Amendments of 1974, Special Projects Act	To encourage the establishment of art programs at the elementary and secondary levels	500,000	State and local educational agencies	OE Arts and Humanities Staff, Office of the Commissioner
PART B—For Strengthening Organizational Resources					
20 Library services (OMB Cat. No. 13.464)	Library Services and Construction Act, Title I	To extend and improve public library services, institutional library services, and library services to physically handicapped persons	49,155,000	State library administrative agencies	OE Office of Libraries and Learning Resources
21 Interlibrary cooperation (OMB Cat. No. 13.465)	Library Services and Construction Act, Title III	To establish and operate cooperative networks of libraries	2,594,000	State library administrative agencies	OE Office of Libraries and learning Resources
22 State administration of NDEA programs (OMB Cat. No. 13.483)	National Defense Education Act, Title III	To strengthen administration in State education agencies for supervisory and related services for NDEA programs in elementary and secondary schools	2,000,000	State education agencies	OE Office of Libraries and Learning Resources
23 School equipment loans (OMB Cat. No. 13.479)	National Defense Education Act, Title III, Sec. 305	To provide interest-bearing loans to private schools to improve instruction of academic subjects	250,000	Nonprofit private elementary and secondary schools	OE Office of Libraries and Learning Resources

TYPE OF ASSISTANCE	AUTHORIZING LEGISLATION	PURPOSE	APPRO-PRIATION (dollars)	WHO MAY APPLY	WHERE TO APPLY
24 Books and instructional materials (OMB Cat. No. 13.480)	National Defense Education Act, Title III	To strengthen instruction of academic subjects in public schools	19,500,000	State education agencies	OE Office of Libraries and Learning Resources
25 Teacher Corps (OMB Cat. No. 13.489)	Education Professions Development Act, Part B-1	To strengthen the educational opportunities available to children in areas having concentrations of low-income families and to encourage colleges and universities to broaden their programs of teacher preparation and to encourage institutions of higher education and local educational agencies to improve programs of training and retraining for teachers and teacher aides	37,500,000	Institutions of higher education, local education agencies and State education agencies	OE Teacher Corps Office
26 Educational broadcasting facilities (OMB Cat. No. 13.413)	Public Broadcasting Act of 1967, as amended	To aid in the acquisition and installation of broadcast equipment for educational radio and TV	12,000,000	Nonprofit agencies, public colleges, State broadcast agencies and education agencies	OE Grant Application Control Center
27 Educational television (OMB Cat. No. 13.541)	Cooperative Research Act	To fund the development and dissemination of educational television programs	7,000,000	Nonprofit agencies, State and local educational agencies	OE Grant Application Control Center
28 Projects in environmental education (OMB Cat. No. 13.522)	Environmental Education Act of 1970 (P.L. 91-516)	To develop environmental and ecological awareness, and problem solving skills through education programs conducted by formal and non-formal educational organizations and institutions	1,900,000	Colleges and universities, postsecondary schools, local and State educational agencies and other public and private nonprofit agencies, institutions and organizations	OE Grant Application Control Center

			(Final action by Congress not completed)	Institutions of higher education, State and local educational agencies, public and private education or community agencies, institutions, and organizations	
29 Alcohol and drug abuse education programs (OMB Cat. No. 13,420)	Alcohol and Drug Abuse Education Act of 1974 (P.L. 93,422)	To organize and train alcohol and drug education leadership teams at State and local levels, to provide technical assistance to these teams, to develop programs and leadership to combat causes of alcohol and drug abuse			OE Division of Drug Education, Nutrition and Health Programs

PART C—For Postsecondary Education Programs

30 Advanced institutional development (OMB Cat. No. 13,454)	Higher Education Act of 1965, Title III, as amended	To assist selected developing institutions enter the mainstream of higher education	58,000,000	Developing institutions with demonstrated progress	OE Divisions of Institutional Development
31 Basic Institutional development (OMB Cat. No. 13,454)	Higher Education Act of 1965, Title III	To provide partial support for cooperative arrangements between developing and established institutions	52,000,000 (includes 32)	Accredited colleges and universities in existence at least five years	OE Division of Institutional Development
32 National teaching fellowships and professors emeriti (OMB Cat. No. 13,454)	Higher Education Act of 1965, Title III	To strengthen the teaching resources of developing institutions	(included in 31)	Colleges, universities, vocational, and proprietary schools	OE Division of Student Support and Special Programs
33 Cooperative education programs (OMB Cat. No. 13,510)	Higher Education Act of 1965, Title IV-D, as amended	To support the planning and implementation of programs alternating periods of full-time study and full-time work	10,750,000	Colleges and universities	OE Division of Training and Facilities
34 National Direct Student Loan Program (OMB Cat. No. 13,471)	Higher Education Act of 1965, Title IV-E, as amended	To assist in setting up funds at institutions of higher education for the purpose of making low-interest loans to graduate and undergraduate students attending at least half-time	329,440,000	Colleges and universities	OE Division of Student Support and Special Programs
35 Cuban student loans (OMB Cat. No. 13,453)	Migration and Refugee Assistance Act	To provide a loan fund to aid Cuban Refugee students	800,000	Colleges and Universities	OE Division of Student Support and Special Programs

TYPE OF ASSISTANCE	AUTHORIZING LEGISLATION	PURPOSE	APPRO-PRIATION (dollars)	WHO MAY APPLY	WHERE TO APPLY
36 Endowments to agriculture and mechanic arts college (OMB Cat. No. 13.453)	Bankhead-Jones and Morrill-Nelson Acts	To support instruction in agriculture and mechanic arts in land-grant colleges	12,200,000	The 69 land-grant colleges	OE Division of Training and Facilities
37 State student incentive grants (OMB Cat. No. 13.548)	Higher Education Act, Title IV	To encourage States to increase their appropriations for grants to needy students or to develop such grant programs where they do not exist (grants are on a matching 50-50 basis)	20,000,000	State education agencies	OE Division of Basic and State Student Grants
38 Postsecondary education innovation and reform (OMB Cat. No. 13.538)	Education Amendments of 1972	To aid postsecondary education in generating reforms in curriculum development, teaching, and administration	11,500,000	Postsecondary institutions and related organizations	Fund for the Improvement of Postsecondary Education (ASE)[4]
39 College work-study (OMB Cat. No. 13.463)	Higher Education Act of 1965, Title IV-C, as amended	To stimulate and promote the part-time employment and post secondary students of great financial need	300,200,000	Colleges, universities, vocational, and proprietary schools	OE Division of Student Support and Special Programs
40 State administration of Higher Education Act Titles VI-A and VII-A programs (OMB Cat. No. 13.550)	Higher Education Act, Title XII	To help States administer programs under Title VI and VII of the Higher Education Act	3,000,000	State commissions that administer academic facilities and instructional equipment programs	OE Division of Training and Facilities
41 University community services programs (OMB Cat. No. 13.491)	Higher Education Act of 1965, Title I	To strengthen higher education capabilities in helping communities solve their problems	14,250,000	Colleges and universities	State agencies or Institutions designated to administer State plans (Information from OE Division of Training and Facilities)

Program	Authority	Purpose	Amount	Eligible	Administering Office
42 College library resources (OMB Cat. No. 13.406)	Higher Education Act of 1965, Title II-A	To strengthen library resources of junior colleges, colleges, universities, and post-secondary vocational schools	9,975,000	Postsecondary Institutions	OE Office of Libraries and Learning Resources
43 Student special services (OMB Cat. No. 13.482)	Higher Education Amendments of 1968, Title I-A	To assist low-income and handicapped students to complete postsecondary education	23,000,000	Accredited institutions of higher learning or consortiums	HEW Regional Offices
44 Veterans cost of instruction (OMB Cat. No. 13.540)	Higher Education Act, Title X	To encourage recruitment and counseling of veterans by postsecondary education institutions	23,750,000	Postsecondary education institutions	OE Veterans Program Branch
45 Supplemental educational opportunity grants (OMB Cat. No. 13.418)	Education Amendments of 1972	To assist students of exceptional financial need to pursue a postsecondary education	240,300,000	Institutions of higher education	OE Division of Student Support and Special Programs
46 Talent Search (OMB Cat. No. 13.488)	Higher Education Act of 1965, Title IV-A, as amended	To assist in identifying and encouraging promising students to complete high school and pursue postsecondary education	6,000,000	Institutions of higher education and combinations of such institutions, public and private nonprofit agencies, and public and private	HEW Regional Offices
47 Undergraduate instructional equipment (OMB Cat. No. 13.518)	Higher Education Act of 1965, Title VI-A	To improve undergraduate instruction	7,500,000	Institutions of higher education, including vocational and technical schools and hospital schools of nursing	OE Office of Libraries and Learning Resources
48 Upward Bound (OMB Cat. No. 13.492)	Higher Education Act of 1965, Title IV-A, as amended	To generate skills and motivation for young people with low-income backgrounds and inadequate high school preparation	38,331,000	Accredited institutions of higher education and secondary or postsecondary schools capable of providing residential facilities	HEW Regional Offices

TYPE OF ASSISTANCE	AUTHORIZING LEGISLATION	PURPOSE	APPROPRIATION (dollars)	WHO MAY APPLY	WHERE TO APPLY
49 Fellowships for higher education personnel (OMB Cat. No. 13.462)	Education Professions Development Act, Part E	To train persons to serve as teachers, administrators, or education specialists in higher education	2,100,000	Institutions of higher education with graduate programs	OE Division of Training and Facilities
50 Educational opportunity centers (OMB Cat. No. 13.543)	Education Amendments of 1972, Title IV	To operate centers that provide assistance to low-income persons desiring to pursue a program of postsecondary education	3,000,000	Institutions of higher education and combinations of such institutions, public and private nonprofit agencies and organizations	OE Division of Student Support and Special Programs
PART D—For the Education of the Handicapped					
51 Deaf-blind centers (OMB Cat. No. 13.445)	Education of the Handicapped Act, Title VI-C (P.L. 91-230)	To provide specialized, intensive educational and therapeutic services to deaf-blind children and their families through regional centers	12,000,000	State education agencies, universities, medical centers, public or nonprofit agencies	OE Bureau of Education for the Handicapped
52 Early education for handicapped children (OMB Cat. No. 13.444)	Education of the Handicapped Act, Title VI-C (P.L. 91-230)	To develop model preschool and early education programs for handicapped children	14,000,000	Public agencies and private nonprofit agencies	OE Bureau of Education for the Handicapped
53 Information and recruitment (OMB Cat. No. 13.452)	Education of the Handicapped Act, Title VI-D (P.L. 91-230)	To encourage the recruitment of educational personnel and the dissemination of information on educational opportunities for the handicapped	500,000	Public agencies and private nonprofit agencies and organizations	OE Bureau of Education for the Handicapped
54 Media services and captioned film loan program-film (OMB Cat. No. 13.446)	Education of the Handicapped Act, Title VI-F	To advance the handicapped through film and other media, including a captioned film loan service for cultural and educational enrichment of the deaf	13,000,000 (includes 55, 56, and 11.22)	State or local public agencies, schools, and organizations which serve the handicapped, their	OE Bureau of Education for the Handicapped

55 Media services and captioned film loan program-centers (OMB Cat. No. 13.446)	Education of the Handicapped Act, Title VI-F	To establish and operate a national center on educational media for the handicapped	(included in 54)	Institutions of higher education	OE Bureau of Education for the Handicapped
56 Media services and captioned film loan program-research (OMB Cat. No. 13.446)	Education of the Handicapped Act, Title VI-F	To contract for research in the use of educational and training films and other educational media for the handicapped and for their production and distribution	(included in 54)	By invitation; requests for proposals published in Commerce Business Daily	OE Bureau of Education for the Handicapped
57 Programs for children with specific learning disabilities (OMB Cat. No. 13.520)	Education for the Handicapped Act, Title VI-G	To provide for research, training of personnel and establishment of model centers for the improvement of education of children with learning disabilities	3,250,000	Institutions of higher education. State and local education agencies, and other public and private nonprofit agencies	OE Bureau of Education for the Handicapped
58 Programs for the Handicapped-aid to States (OMB Cat. No. 13.449)	Education of the Handicapped Act, Title VI-B	To strengthen educational and related services of handicapped children	100,000,000	State education agencies	OE Bureau of Education for the Handicapped
59 Programs for the handicapped in State-supported schools (OMB Cat. No. 13.427)	Elementary and Secondary Education Act, Title I	To strengthen programs for children in State-supported schools	88,927,000	Eligible State agencies	OE Bureau of Education for the Handicapped
60 Personnel training for the education of the handicapped (OMB Cat. 13.451)	Education of the Handicapped Act, Title VI-D	To prepare and inform teachers and others who educate handicapped children	37,700,000 (includes 61)	State education agencies, colleges, universities, and other appropriate nonprofit agencies	OE Bureau of Education for the Handicapped

parents, employers, or potential employers

TYPE OF ASSISTANCE	AUTHORIZING LEGISLATION	PURPOSE	APPRO-PRIATION (dollars)	WHO MAY APPLY	WHERE TO APPLY
61 Training of physical education and recreation personnel for handicapped children (OMB Cat. No. 13.448)	Education of the Handicapped Act, Title VI-D	To train physical education and recreation personnel to work with the handicapped	(included in 60)	Institutions of higher education	OE Bureau of Education for the Handicapped
62 Regional education programs for the handicapped (OMB Cat. No. 13.560)	Education of the Handicapped Act, Part C, Sec. 616	To make grants or contracts with institutions for the development and operation of specially designed or modified programs of vocational, technical, postsecondary, or adult education for deaf or other handicapped persons	575,000	Institutions of higher education, junior and community colleges, vocational and technical institutes	OE Bureau of Education for the Handicapped
63 Handicapped regional resource centers (OMB Cat. No. 13.450)	Education of the Handicapped Act, Title I	To establish regional resource centers which provide advice and technical services to educators for improving education of handicapped children	7,087,000	Institutions of higher education, State education agencies or combinations of such, including local education agencies	OE Bureau of Education for the Handicapped
64 Supplementary educational centers and services, counseling guidance, and testing for the handicapped	Elementary and Secondary Education Act, Title III	To assist in providing vitally needed educational services, to support local innovative and exemplary projects and programs of guidance, counseling and testing	16,348,331 (15 percent set aside)	State education agencies	OE Bureau of Education for the Handicapped
PART E—For the Support of Overseas Educational Program					
65 Consultant services of foreign curriculum specialists (OMB Cat. No. 13.439)	Mutual Educational and Cultural Exchange Act and Agricultural Trade Development and	To support visits by foreign consultants to improve and develop resources for foreign language and area studies	120,000 (plus foreign currency)	Colleges, consortiums, local and State education agencies, nonprofit education organizations	OE Division of International Education

	Assistance Act, P.L. 83-480				
66 Group projects abroad for non-Western language and area studies (OMB Cat. No. 13.440)	Mutual Educational and Cultural Exchange Act and P.L. 83-480 (in excess foreign currency countries)	To improve programs of international studies	2,068,494[5] (includes 67)	Colleges, universities, consortiums, local and State education agencies, nonprofit education organizations	OE Division of International Education
67 Institutional cooperative research abroad for comparative and cross-cultural studies (OMB Cat. No. 13,438)	Agricultural Trade Development and Assistance Act of 1954, P.L. 83-480	To promote research on educational problems of mutual concern to American and foreign educators	(included in 66)	College, universities, consortiums, local and State education agencies, nonprofit education organizations	OE Division of International Education
68 Foreign language and area studies centers (OMB Cat. No. 13,435)	National Defense Education Act of 1958, Title VI	To provide financial assistance to institutions of higher education for the establishment and operation of centers for the teaching of any modern foreign language and area studies	6,800,000	Colleges and universities	OE Division of International Education
PART F—For Occupational, Adult, Vocational, and Career Education					
69 Adult education (OMB Cat. No. 13.400)	Adult Education Act of 1966, as amended	To provide adult basic education programs, through 12th grade competency	67,500,000	State education agencies	OE Division of Adult Education
70 Vocational education programs (OMB Cat. No. 13.493)	Vocational Education Act of 1963, Part B, as amended	To maintain, extend and improve vocational education programs, to develop programs in new occupations	428,139,455[6]	Local education agencies	State vocational education agencies

TYPE OF ASSISTANCE	AUTHORIZING LEGISLATION	PURPOSE	APPRO-PRIATION (dollars)	WHO MAY APPLY	WHERE TO APPLY
71 Consumer and homemaking education (OMB Cat. No. 13.494)	Vocational Education Act of 1963, Part F, as amended	To assist States in conducting training programs in consumer and homemaking education, especially in economically depressed or high unemployment areas	35,994,000	Local education agencies	State vocational education agencies
72 Cooperative education for vocational students (OMB Cat. No. 13.495)	Vocational Education Act of 1963, Part G, as amended	To assist the States in conducting vocational education programs designed to prepare students for employment through cooperative work-study arrangements	19,500,000	Local education agencies	State vocational education agencies
73 Work-study programs for vocational students (OMB Cat. No. 13.501)	Vocational Education Act of 1963, Part H, as amended	To provide work opportunities for full-time disadvantaged vocational education students	9,849,000	Local education agencies	State vocational education agencies
74 Vocational programs for persons with special needs (OMB Cat. No. 13.499)	Vocational Education Act of 1963, Section 102(b), as amended	To provide vocational education programs for persons with academic, socio-economic or social handicaps which prevent them from succeeding in the regular program	20,000,000	Local education agencies	State vocational education agencies
75 Bilingual vocational training (OMB Cat. No. 13.558)	Vocational Education Act of 1963, Part J, as amended	To assist in conducting bilingual vocational training programs to insure that vocational training programs are available to all individuals who desire and need such training	2,800,000	State agencies, local education agencies, postsecondary educational institutions, and other nonprofit organizations	OE Bureau of Occupational and Adult Education
76 Career education (OMB Cat. No. 13.554)	Education Amendments of 1974, Special Projects Act	To demonstrate the most effective methods and techniques in career education and to develop exemplary career education models	10,000,000	State and local education agencies, institutions of higher education, and other nonprofit	OE Office of Career Education

PART G—For Desegregation Assistance

				organizations and agencies	
77 Desegregation assistance, special programs and projects (OMB Cat. No. 13.529)	Education Amendments of 1972, Title VII (Emergency School Aid Act), Section 708(b)	To promote aid for community-based special programs and projects in support of school district desegregation plans	(Appropriation level pending final Congressional action)	Nonprofit organizations (public or private)	HEW Regional Offices
78 Desegregation assistance, basic grants (OMB Cat. No. 13.525)	Education Amendments of 1972, Title VII (Emergency School Aid Act), Section 706(a)	To provide aid to desegregating school districts for educational programs	(Same as 77)	Local public school districts	HEW Regional Offices
79 Desegregation assistance, pilot projects (OMB Cat. No. 13.526)	Education Amendments of 1972, Title VII (Emergency School Aid Act), Section 706(b)	To help desegregating school districts provide special educational assistance to overcome minority group isolation	(Same as 77)	Local public school districts	HEW Regional Offices
80 Desegregation assistance, bilingual programs (OMB Cat. No. 13.528)	Education Amendments of 1972, Title VII (Emergency School Aid Act), Section 706(b)	To help desegregating school districts provide bilingual-bicultural programs for children of limited English speaking ability	(Same as 77)	Local public school districts and private nonprofit organizations	HEW Regional Offices
81 Desegregation assistance, educational TV (OMB Cat. No. 15.530)	Education Amendments of 1972, Title VII (Emergency School Aid Act), Section 711	To develop and produce integrated children's educational television programs	(Same as 77)	Public or private nonprofit organizations, agencies or institutions	OE Grant Application Control Center

TYPE OF ASSISTANCE	AUTHORIZING LEGISLATION	PURPOSE	APPRO- PRIATION (dollars)	WHO MAY APPLY	WHERE TO APPLY
82 Desegregation assistance, special programs (OMB Cat. No. 13.532)	Education Amendments of 1972, Title VII, (Emergency School Aid Act) Section 708(a)	To support efforts of special merit serving ESAA aims	(Same as 77)	Local public school districts, public organizations, and (for mathematics projects) private nonprofit organizations	OE Grant Application Control Center
83 Desegregation assistance to local education agencies (OMB Cat. No. 13.405)	Civil Rights Act of 1964, Title IV	To aid school districts in hiring advisory specialists to train employees and provide technical assistance in matters related to desegregation on the basis of race, color, religion, sex, or national origin	267,700,000 (includes 84 and 85)	School districts	HEW Regional Offices
84 Desegregation assistance to teacher institutes (OMB Cat. No. 13.405)	Civil Rights Act of 1964, Title IV	To improve the ability of school personnel to deal with school desegregation problems	(included in 83)	Colleges and universities	HEW Regional Offices
85 Desegregation assistance to general assistance centers and State education agencies (OMB Cat. No. 13.405)	Civil Rights Act of 1964, Title IV	To provide technical assistance for school desegregation activities as described in 83; also desegregation problems associated with non-English speaking student populations	(included in 83)	Colleges, universities, and State education agencies	HEW Regional Offices or OE Grant Application Control Center
GROUP II: TO INDIVIDUALS—FOR TEACHER AND OTHER PROFESSIONAL TRAINING, AND STUDENT ASSISTANCE					
1 Basic educational opportunity grants (OMB Cat. No. 13.539)	Education Amendments of 1972	To provide financial assistance to post-secondary students at the undergraduate level	660,000,000	Postsecondary education students	P.O. Box G, Iowa City, IA, 52240

2 College work-study (OMB Cat. No. 13.463)	Higher Education Act of 1965, Title IV-C, as amended	To stimulate and promote the part-time employment of postsecondary students of great financial need	(See 1, 39)	Graduate, undergraduate, and vocational students enrolled at least half-time in approved educational institutions	Participating institutions (information from OE Division of Student Support and Special Programs)
3 Cuban student loans (OMB Cat. No. 13.409)	Migration and Refugee Assistance Act	To provide loans to needy Cuban refugee students	(See 1, 35)	Cubans who became refugees after January 1, 1959	Participating institutions (information from OE Division of Student Support and Special Programs)
4 Direct student loans (OMB Cat. No. 13.471)	Higher Education Act of 1965, as amended, Title IV-E	To provide low-interest loans to postsecondary students	(See 1, 34)	Graduate and undergraduate students enrolled on at least a half-time basis	Participating institutions (information from OE Division of Student Support)
5 Educational development (for educators from other countries)	Mutual Educational and Cultural Exchange Act	To provide opportunity for educators to observe U.S. methods, curriculum, and organization on elementary, secondary and higher education levels	360,000	Educators from abroad (including administrators, teacher-trainers, education ministry officials)	OE Division of International Education
6 Fellowships abroad for doctoral dissertation research in foreign language and area studies (OMB Cat. No. 13.441)	Mutual Educational and Cultural Exchange Act	To develop research knowledge and international studies capabilities	1,371,000	Prospective teachers of language and area studies	Graduate dean at participating institutions (information from OE Division of International Education)

TYPE OF ASSISTANCE	AUTHORIZING LEGISLATION	PURPOSE	APPRO-PRIATION (dollars)	WHO MAY APPLY	WHERE TO APPLY
7 Fellowships for higher education personnel (OMB Cat. No. 13.462)	Education Professions Development Act,	To train persons to serve as teachers, administrators, or education specialists in higher education	(See 1, 49)	Graduate students	Participating institutions (Information from OE Division of Training and Facilities)
8 Fellowship opportunities abroad (OMB Cat. No. 13.438)	Mutual Educational and Cultural Exchange Act, and P.L. 83-480 (in excess foreign currency countries)	To promote instruction in international studies through grants for graduate and faculty projects	400,000[5]	Faculty in foreign languages and area studies	Institutions of higher education at which applicants are enrolled or employed (information from OE Division of International Education
9 National teaching fellowships and professors emeriti (OMB Cat. No. 13.454)	Higher Education Act of 1965, Title III	To strengthen the teaching resources of developing institutions	(See 1, 30)	Highly qualified graduate students or junior faculty members from established institutions and retired scholars	(Information from OE Division of Institutional Development)
10 State student incentive grants (OMB Cat. No. 13.548)	Higher Education Act, Title IV	To encourage States to increase their appropriations for students or to develop such grant programs where they do not exist—grants are on a 50-50, matching funds basis	(See 1, 37)	Postsecondary education students	State education agencies (information from OE Division of Basic and State Student Grants)
11 Supplemental Educational opportunity grants (OMB Cat. No. 13.418)	Educational Amendments of 1972	To assist students of exceptional financial need	(See 1, 45)	Postsecondary education students	Participating educational institutions (information from OE Division of

Program	Authority	Objective	Amount	Eligible recipients	Student Support and Special Programs
12 Teacher exchange (OMB Cat. No. 13.437)	Mutual Education and Cultural Exchange Act and P.L. 83-480	To promote international understanding and professional competence by exchange of teachers between the U.S. and foreign nations	1,320,000 (includes funds contributed by foreign governments on a cost sharing basis)	Elementary and secondary school teachers, college instructors, and assistant professors	OE Division of International Education
13 College teacher graduate fellowships (OMB Cat. No. 13.407)	Higher Education Act, Title IX	To increase the number of qualified college teachers	4,000,000	Prospective college teachers working toward doctoral degrees	Participating institutions (information from OE Division of Training and Facilities)
14 Librarian training (OMB Cat. No. 13.468)	Higher Education Act, Title II-B	To increase opportunities for training in librarianship	2,000,000	Prospective and/or experienced librarians and information specialists	Participating institutions (information from OE Office of Libraries and Learning Resources)
15 Vocational education personnel development awards (OMB Cat. No. 13.503)	Higher Education Act of 1965, Title V, as amended	To meet State needs for qualified vocational education personnel by making awards to educators and by making institutional awards to develop such programs	9,000,000	Current and prospective vocational educators	State vocational education agencies
16 Vocational education professional personnel development for States (OMB Cat. No. 13.504)	Higher Education Act of 1965, Title V, as amended	To strengthen education programs authorized by the Vocational Education Amendments of 1968, and to improve the instruction and administration of vocational education at all levels	(included in 15)	Professional personnel in vocational education	State vocational education agencies

TYPE OF ASSISTANCE	AUTHORIZING LEGISLATION	PURPOSE	APPRO-PRIATION (dollars)	WHO MAY APPLY	WHERE TO APPLY
17 Foreign language and area studies fellowships (OMB Cat. No. 13.434)	National Defense Education Act of 1958, Title VI	To pay stipends to individuals undergoing training in any modern foreign language	3,600,000	Graduate students of languages	OE Division of International Education
18 Public service career fellowships (OMB Cat. No. 13.555)	Higher Education Act of 1965, Title IX, Parts A and C	To prepare students for entrance into the service of State, local, or Federal governments and to attract such students to the public service	4,000,000	Students who hold Bachelor's degrees and wish to pursue a public service career	Participating institutions (information from OE Division of Training and Facilities)
19 Domestic mining and mineral and mineral-fuel conservation fellowships (OMB Cat. No. 13.567)	Higher Education Act of 1965, Title IX, Part D	To assist graduate students from advanced study in domestic mining and mineral and mineral-fuel conservation, including gas, oil, coal, shale, and uranium	1,500,000	Advanced degree candidates	Participating institutions (information from OE Division of Training and Facilities)
20 Guaranteed student loan program (OMB Cat. No. 13.460)	Higher Education Act of 1965, Title IV B, as amended	To encourage private commercial institutions and organizations to make loans for educational purposes to postsecondary students	(private capital is used for these loans)	Students accepted for enrollment on at least a half-time basis in an eligible postsecondary educational institution	Private lenders
21 Ellender fellowships	P.L. 92-506	To assist the Close Up Foundation of Washington, D.C. to carry out its program of increasing understanding of the Federal Government among secondary school students and the communities they represent	500,000	Economically disadvantaged secondary school students and secondary school teachers	The Close Up Foundation, 1660 L Street, N.W. Washington, D.C. 20036
22 Media services and captioned films training grants (OMB Cat. No. 13.446)	Education of the Handicapped Act, Title VI-F (P.L. 91-230)	To contract for training persons in the use of educational media for the handicapped	(See 1, 54)	Persons who will use captioned film equipment	OE Bureau of Education for the Handicapped

23 Training teachers for the handicapped (OMB Cat. No. 13.451)	Education of the Handicapped Act, Title VI-D (P.L. 91-230)	To improve the quality and increase the supply of educational personnel trained to work with handicapped children	(See 1, 60)	Qualified individuals with varying levels of education	Participating institutions (information from OE Bureau of Education for the Handicapped, Division of Personnel Preparation)
24 Training of physical education and recreation personnel for handicapped children (OMB Cat. No. 13.448)	Education of the Handicapped Act, Title VI-D (P.L. 91-230)	To train physical education and recreation personnel for the handicapped	(See 1, 61)	Qualified individuals at undergraduate and graduate levels	Participating institutions (information from OE Bureau of Education for the Handicapped, Division of Personnel Preparation)
25 Teacher Corps project grants (OMB Cat. No. 13.489)	Education Professions Development Act, Part B-1	To improve the quality of instruction available to disadvantaged children	(See 1, 25)	Qualified undergraduate and graduate students	Participating institutions (information from OE Teacher Corps Office)

GROUP III: FOR RESEARCH

1 Research and demonstration for handicapped (OMB Cat. No. 13.443)	Education of the Handicapped Act, Title VI	To improve the education of handicapped children through research and demonstration projects	9,341,000	Institutions of higher education State or local education agencies, public or private educational or research agencies and organizations	OE Bureau of Education for the Handicapped

	TYPE OF ASSISTANCE	AUTHORIZING LEGISLATION	PURPOSE	APPRO-PRIATION (dollars)	WHO MAY APPLY	WHERE TO APPLY
2	Handicapped physical education and recreation research (OMB Cat. No. 13.447)	Education of the Handicapped Act, Title VI	To improve physical education and recreation programs for handicapped children through research and demonstration projects	(See 1, 61)	Institutions of higher education, State or local education agencies, public or private educational or research agencies and organizations	OE Bureau of Education for the Handicapped
3	Vocational education curriculum development (OMB Cat. No. 13.498)	Vocational Education Act of 1963, as amended, Part I	To develop standards for curriculum development in all occupational fields and dissemination of materials for use in teaching occupational subjects	1,000,000	State and local education agencies, private institutions and organizations	OE Grant Application Control Center
4	Vocational education research, developing new careers and occupations, (OMB Cat. No. 13.498)	Vocational Education Act of 1963, as amended, Part C	To develop new vocational education careers and to disseminate information about them	9,000,000	Education agencies, private institutions, and organizations	OE Grant Application Control Center
5	Vocational education research, meeting vocational needs of youth (OMB Cat. No. 13.498)	Vocational Education Act of 1963, as amended, Part C	To develop programs that meet the special vocational needs of youths with academic and socio-economic handicaps	9,000,000	State boards of vocational education	HEW Regional Offices
6	Vocational education research, innovative projects (OMB Cat. No. 13.502)	Vocational Education Act of 1963, as amended, Part D	To develop, establish and operate exemplary and innovative projects to serve as models for vocational education programs	8,000,000	State boards of vocational education	Bureau of Occupational and Adult Education, Division of Research and Demonstration
7	Vocational education research, relating school curriculums to careers	Vocational Education Act of 1963, as amended, Part D	To stimulate the development of new methods for relating school work to occupational fields and public education to	8,000,000	State boards of education local education agencies, public and private	HEW Regional Offices

[OMB Cat. No. 13.502]		manpower agencies		agencies and institutions	OE Office of Libraries and Learning Resources
8 Library demonstrations (OMB Cat. No. 13.475)	Higher Education Act Title II	To promote library and information science research and demonstrations	1,000,000	Institutions of higher education and other public or private nonprofit agencies, institutions, and organizations	OE Office of Libraries and Learning Resources
9 Foreign language and area studies research (OMB Cat. No. 13.436)	National Defense Education Act, Title VI	To improve foreign language and area studies through support of research, experimentation, development of specialized instructional materials and studies	860,000	Institutions of higher education, State education agencies, other educational and professional organizations	OE Division of International Education
GROUP IV: FOR CONSTRUCTION					
1 Public schools (OMB Cat. No. 13.477)	School Aid to Federally Impacted and Major Disaster Areas (P.L. 815)	Aid school districts in providing minimum school facilities in federally impacted and disaster areas	20,000,000	Local school districts	HEW Regional Offices
2 Vocational facilities (OMB Cat. No. 23.012)	Appalachian Regional Development Act of 1965	Construct area vocational education facilities in the Appalachian region	24,000,000	State education agencies in the Appalachian region	OE Division of Vocational and Technical Education

ADDITIONAL PROGRAMS—The following are new programs established by the Special Projects Act, Education Amendments of 1974 (P.L. 93-380) and will be included for the first time in the FY 1976 budget.

1 Metric education (OMB Cat. No. 13.561)	Education Amendments of 1974 (Special Projects Act, Sec. 403)	To encourage educational agencies to prepare students to use the metric system of measurement	(To Be Determined)	State and local educational agencies, institutions of higher education, public and private nonprofit agencies, organizations, and institutions	OE Bureau of Occupational and Adult Education

	TYPE OF ASSISTANCE	AUTHORIZING LEGISLATION	PURPOSE	APPRO-PRIATION (dollars)	WHO MAY APPLY	WHERE TO APPLY
2	Gifted and talented children (OMB Cat. No. 13.562)	Education Amendments of 1974, Special Projects Act, Sec. 404	To develop programs to meet special educational needs of gifted and talented children; to train leadership personnel to meet those needs	(To Be Determined)	State and local educational agencies, institutions of higher education, appropriate nonprofit institutions or agencies	OE Bureau of Education for the Handicapped
3	Community schools (OMB Cat. No. 13.563)	Education Amendments of 1974, Special Projects Act, Sec. 405	To assist State and local educational agencies in establishing community schools; to train personnel to plan and operate community education programs	(To Be Determined)	State and local educational agencies, institutions of higher education	OE Bureau of Occupational and Adult Education
4	Consumers education (OMB Cat. No. 13.564)	Education Amendments of 1974, Special Projects Act, Sec. 407	To support research and development and pilot projects designed to provide consumer education to the public	(To Be Determined)	State and local educational agencies, institutions of higher education, public libraries, public or private nonprofit organizations or agencies	OE Bureau of Occupational and Adult Education
5	Women's educational equity (OMB Cat. No. 13.565)	Education Amendments of 1974, Special Projects Act, Sec. 408	To carry out activities at all levels of education aimed at providing women's educational equity and to train personnel to conduct such activities	(To Be Determined)	Public agencies and private nonprofit organization	OE Women's Program Staff Office of the Commissioner

[1] Refers to identifying number as it appears in the Office of Management and Budget Catalog of Federal Domestic Assistance

[2] $16,348,325 earmarked for special education

[3] Includes ten percent set aside for non-LEAs (local education agencies)

[4] Administered by the Assistant Secretary for Education, another component of the Education Division

[5] Includes appropriated excess foreign currency

[6] At least ten percent for handicapped

Appendix VI:

Estimated Materials Acquisitions by U.S. Libraries 1972-73 to 1978-79
(MILLIONS OF DOLLARS AND UNITS)

Figures in italics represent percentage changes from previous year; parentheses show decline

	1972-73		1973-74			
	Dollars	Units	Dollars		Units	
College and University Libraries						
Books (Total)	154.6	15.21	168.7	*9.1*	14.55	*(4.3)*
Domestic	82.4	6.21	88.6	*7.5*	6.08	*(2.1)*
Imports	56.9	5.58	63.1	*10.9*	5.23	*(6.3)*
Government and Special	15.3	3.40	17.0	*11.1*	3.74	*(4.7)*
Periodicals	106.6	1.64	118.4	*11.1*	1.58	*(3.7)*
Audiovisuals	19.4	1.17	21.4	*10.3*	1.08	*(7.7)*
Microform	19.3		21.5	*11.4*		*(1.6)*
Binding	22.8		25.1	*10.1*		*.1*
Total College and Univ. Libraries	322.7		355.1	*10.0*		
Public Libraries						
Books (Total)	136.9	24.26	153.3	*12.0*	24.55	*1.2*
Domestic	128.5	22.45	143.7	*11.8*	22.73	*1.2*
Imports	3.1	.30	3.5	*12.9*	.29	*(3.3)*
Government and Special	5.3	1.51	6.1	*15.1*	1.53	*1.3*
Periodicals	16.2	.58	18.3	*13.0*	.57	*(1.7)*
Audiovisuals	16.7	1.01	18.8	*17.6*	.95	*(5.9)*
Microform	6.0		6.6	*10.0*		*(3.0)*
Binding	6.1		6.7	*9.8*		*(.2)*
Total Public Libraries	181.9		203.7	*12.0*		
Special Libraries						
Books (Total)	68.1	6.58	77.5	*13.8*	6.51	*(1.1)*
Domestic	38.4	2.60	43.4	*.13.0*	2.59	*(.4)*
Imports	22.7	2.23	26.1	*14.6*	2.18	*(2.2)*
Government and Special	7.0	1.75	8.0	*14.3*	1.74	*(.6)*
Periodicals	58.8	.90	68.1	*15.8*	.91	*1.1*
Audiovisuals	9.5	.58	11.0	*15.7*	.56	*(3.4)*
Microform	11.7		13.3	*13.7*		*.7*
Binding	11.3		12.4	*9.7*		*(.3)*
Total Special Libraries	159.4		182.3	*14.4*		
School Libraries						
Books	140.6	39.08	154.9	*10.2*	39.29	*.5*
Periodicals	18.4	.80	20.6	*12.0*	.78	*(2.5)*
Audiovisuals	149.7	9.07	173.8	*16.1*	8.78	*(3.1)*
Microform	4.9		5.4	*10.2*		*(2.8)*
Binding	1.0		1.1	*10.0*		*0.0*
Total School Libraries	314.6		355.8	*13.1*		
All Libraries	978.6		1,096.9	*12.1*		

	1974-75				1975-76			
	Dollars		Units		Dollars		Units	
College and University Libraries								
Books (Total)	174.7	3.6	13.10	(10.0)	180.4	3.3	12.33	(5.9)
Domestic	91.4	3.2	5.62	(8.2)	94.4	3.3	5.38	(4.3)
Imports	65.6	4.0	4.60	(12.0)	67.6	3.0	4.24	(7.8)
Government and Special	17.7	4.1	2.88	(11.1)	18.4	4.0	2.71	(5.9)
Periodicals	123.2	4.1	1.42	(10.1)	129.3	4.7	1.33	(6.3)
Audiovisuals	21.8	1.8	.93	(13.9)	22.6	3.7	.89	(4.3)
Microform	22.1	2.8		(12.2)	23.4	5.9		(1.6)
Binding	26.1	3.4		(6.6)	28.2	8.0		0.0
Total College and Univ. Libraries	367.9	3.6			383.9	4.3		
Public Libraries								
Books (Total)	165.2	7.8	24.53	(.1)	175.2	6.1	24.68	.6
Domestic	154.4	7.4	22.74	0.0	163.6	6.0	22.88	.6
Imports	3.9	11.4	.27	(6.9)	4.4	12.8	.28	1.0
Government and Special	6.9	13.1	1.52	(.7)	7.2	4.3	1.52	0.0
Periodicals	20.9	14.2	.57	0.0	23.0	10.0	.57	0.0
Audiovisuals	21.6	14.9	.93	(2.1)	23.6	9.2	.93	0.0
Microform	7.4	12.1		(2.9)	8.0	8.1		.6
Binding	7.3	9.0		(1.0)	7.9	8.2		.2
Total Public Libraries	222.4	9.2			237.7	6.9		
Special Libraries								
Books (Total)	84.9	9.5	6.21	(4.6)	90.9	7.1	6.08	(2.1)
Domestic	47.3	9.0	2.50	(3.5)	50.4	6.6	2.46	(1.6)
Imports	28.7	10.0	2.01	(7.8)	31.3	9.1	1.96	(2.5)
Government and Special	8.9	11.3	1.70	(2.3)	9.2	3.4	1.66	(2.5)
Periodicals	75.1	10.3	.86	(5.5)	81.1	8.0	.84	(2.3)
Audiovisuals	12.2	10.9	.52	(7.1)	13.0	6.5	.51	(1.9)
Microform	14.7	11.1		(3.9)	15.6	6.1		(2.2)
Binding	13.1	5.6		(4.4)	13.8	5.3		(.8)
Total Special Libraries	200.0	9.7			214.4	7.2		
School Libraries								
Books	153.5	(.9)	36.43	(7.3)	150.0	(2.3)	33.92	(6.9)
Periodicals	20.2	(1.9)	.67	(14.1)	19.8	(2.0)	.60	(10.4)
Audiovisuals	166.6	(4.1)	7.13	(18.8)	163.3	(2.0)	6.42	(10.0)
Microform	5.3	(1.8)		(16.8)	5.2	(1.9)		(9.4)
Binding	1.0	(9.0)		(19.0)	1.0	(2.0)		(10.1)
Total School Libraries	346.6	(2.6)			339.3	(2.1)		
All Libraries	1,136.9	3.6			1,175.3	3.4		

	1976-77				1977-78			
	Dollars		Units		Dollars		Units	
College and University Libraries								
Books (Total)	192.5	*6.0*	12.41	*.6*	205.4	*6.7*	12.52	*.9*
Domestic	100.0	*5.9*	5.38	*0.0*	105.9	*5.9*	5.39	*.2*
Imports	73.0	*8.0*	4.24	*0.0*	78.8	*7.9*	4.31	*1.7*
Government and Special	19.5	*6.0*	2.79	*3.0*	20.7	*6.1*	2.82	*1.1*
Periodicals	140.3	*8.5*	1.34	*.7*	155.7	*11.0*	1.38	*3.0*
Audiovisuals	24.2	*7.1*	.90	*1.1*	26.2	*8.3*	.92	*2.2*
Microform	25.0	*6.8*		*1.3*	27.5	*10.0*		*5.0*
Binding	30.1	*6.7*		*0.0*	32.5	*8.0*		*2.0*
Total College and Univ. Libraries	412.1	*7.3*			447.3	*8.5*		
Public Libraries								
Books (Total)	189.8	*8.3*	25.51	*3.4*	207.6	*9.4*	26.57	*4.2*
Domestic	177.4	*8.4*	23.69	*3.5*	194.1	*9.4*	24.69	*4.2*
Imports	4.8	*9.1*	.28	*1.1*	5.3	*10.4*	.29	*3.6*
Government and Special	7.6	*5.5*	1.54	*1.3*	8.2	*7.9*	6.59	*3.2*
Periodicals	24.8	*7.8*	.57	*0.0*	27.5	*10.8*	.60	*5.2*
Audiovisuals	25.5	*8.1*	.94	*1.1*	28.3	*11.0*	.99	*5.3*
Microform	8.6	*7.5*		*2.0*	9.5	*10.5*		*5.5*
Binding	8.5	*7.5*		*.8*	9.2	*8.2*		*2.2*
Total Public Libraries	257.2	*8.2*			282.1	*9.7*		
Special Libraries								
Books (Total)	98.6	*8.5*	6.16	*1.3*	107.8	*9.3*	6.43	*4.4*
Domestic	54.9	*8.9*	2.50	*1.6*	59.8	*8.9*	2.58	*3.2*
Imports	33.9	*8.3*	1.97	*.5*	37.1	*9.4*	2.03	*3.0*
Government and Special	9.8	*6.5*	1.69	*1.8*	10.9	*11.2*	1.82	*7.7*
Periodicals	90.2	*11.2*	.86	*2.4*	100.9	*11.9*	.89	*3.5*
Audiovisuals	13.8	*6.1*	.51	*0.0*	15.3	*10.9*	.54	*5.9*
Microform	16.5	*5.8*		*.3*	18.3	*10.9*		*5.9*
Binding	14.6	*5.8*		*(.9)*	15.9	*8.9*		*3.9*
Total Special Libraries	233.7	*9.0*			258.2	*10.5*		
School Libraries								
Books	154.7	*3.1*	33.36	*(1.7)*	161.3	*4.3*	33.23	*(1.0)*
Periodicals	20.5	*3.5*	.59	*(1.6)*	21.3	*3.9*	.57	*(3.4)*
Audiovisuals	168.5	*3.2*	6.24	*(2.8)*	176.9	*5.0*	6.21	*(.5)*
Microform	5.3	*1.9*		*(3.6)*	5.5	*3.8*		*(1.2)*
Binding	1.0	*2.5*		*(4.2)*	1.0	*3.6*		*(2.4)*
Total School Libraries	350.0	*3.2*			366.0	*4.6*		
All Libraries	1,253.0	*6.6*			1,353.6	*8.0*		

	1978-79			% change 1972-73	
	Dollars		Units	Dollars	Units
College and University Libraries					
Books (Total)	221.9	*8.0*	12.83	*1.0*	43.5	(15.6)
Domestic	112.7	*6.4*	5.44	*.9*	36.8	(12.4)
Imports	86.6	*10.0*	4.45	*3.2*	52.2	(20.2)
Government and Special	22.6	*9.2*	2.94	*3.2*	47.7	(13.5)
Periodicals	174.4	*12.0*	1.44	*4.3*	63.6	(12.2)
Audiovisuals	28.8	*9.9*	.96	*4.3*	48.5	(17.9)
Microform	30.5	*10.9*		*5.9*	58.0	(4.3)
Binding	35.1	*8.0*		*2.0*	53.9	(3.0)
Total College and Univ. Libraries	490.7	*9.7*			52.1	
Public Libraries					
Books (Total)	228.3	*10.0*	27.82	*4.7*	66.8	14.7
Domestic	213.5	*10.0*	25.84	*4.7*	66.1	15.1
Imports	5.8	*9.4*	.30	*3.4*	87.1	0.0
Government and Special	9.0	*9.7*	1.68	*5.7*	69.8	11.3
Periodicals	30.3	*10.2*	.62	*3.3*	87.0	6.8
Audiovisuals	31.0	*9.5*	1.03	*4.0*	85.6	2.0
Microform	10.5	*10.5*		*5.5*	75.0	13.9
Binding	10.0	*8.6*		*2.6*	63.9	4.7
Total Public Libraries	310.1	*9.9*			70.5	
Special Libraries					
Books (Total)	118.4	*9.8*	6.68	*3.9*	73.9	1.5
Domestic	65.7	*9.9*	2.66	*3.1*	71.1	2.3
Imports	40.8	*10.0*	2.10	*3.4*	79.7	(5.8)
Government and Special	11.9	*9.2*	1.92	*5.5*	70.0	9.7
Periodicals	112.0	*11.1*	.93	*4.5*	90.5	3.3
Audiovisuals	16.9	*10.5*	.56	*3.7*	77.9	(3.4)
Microform	20.3	*10.9*		*5.9*	73.5	6.7
Binding	17.5	*10.0*		*4.0*	54.9	(2.1)
Total Special Libraries	285.1	*10.4*			78.9	
School Libraries					
Books	172.7	*7.1*	34.05	*2.5*	22.8	(12.9)
Periodicals	22.8	*7.0*	.58	*1.8*	23.9	(27.5)
Audiovisuals	190.2	*7.5*	6.34	*2.1*	27.1	(30.1)
Microform	5.8	*5.5*		*.5*	18.4	(30.3)
Binding	1.0	*6.0*		*0.0*	11.1	(32.0)
Total School Libraries	392.5	*7.2*			24.8	
All Libraries	1,478.4	*9.2*			51.1	

Appendix VII:

Estimated Acquisitions by U.S. Libraries of Domestically Published Books
1972-73 to 1978-79
(MILLIONS OF DOLLARS AND UNITS)

Figures in italics represent percentage changes from previous year; parentheses show decline

	1972-73		1973-74			
	Dollars	Units	Dollars		Units	
College and University Libraries						
Trade	36.3	3.02	39.4	*8.5*	2.97	*(1.7)*
Technical and Scientific	9.8	.58	10.8	*10.2*	.55	*(5.2)*
Business and Other Professional	10.3	.73	11.3	*9.7*	.73	*0.0*
Medical	10.3	.35	5.8	*9.4*	.32	*(8.6)*
University Press	12.3	1.06	12.4	*.8*	1.05	*(.9)*
Subscription Reference	4.1	.01	4.3	*4.9*	.01	*(6.4)*
Other	4.3	.46	4.6	*7.0*	.45	*(2.2)*
Total College and Univ. Libraries	82.4	6.21	88.6	*7.5*	6.08	*(2.1)*
Public Libraries						
Adult Trade Hardbound	58.4	6.38	66.5	*13.8*	6.55	*2.6*
Adult Trade Paperbound	2.8	1.27	3.2	*14.2*	1.23	*(3.1)*
Juvenile	29.2	8.34	31.0	*6.1*	8.37	*.4*
Professional	18.3	1.22	21.0	*14.7*	1.20	*(1.6)*
Mass Market Paperback	4.3	4.30	4.9	*14.0*	4.45	*3.5*
Subscription Reference	7.2	.03	8.0	*11.1*	.03	*0.0*
Other	8.3	.91	9.1	*9.6*	.90	*(1.1)*
Total Public Libraries	128.5	22.45	143.7	*11.8*	22.73	*1.2*
Special Libraries						
Trade	2.9	.29	3.2	*10.3*	.29	*0.0*
Religious	2.0	.29	2.2	*10.0*	.30	*3.4*
Technical and Scientific	12.1	.72	14.0	*15.7*	.71	*(1.4)*
Business and Other Professional	8.7	.62	9.7	*12.0*	.62	*0.0*
Medical	9.2	.61	10.7	*16.3*	.60	*(1.6)*
Other	3.3	.07	3.6	*9.1*	.07	*(.9)*
Total Special Libraries	38.4	2.60	43.4	*13.0*	2.59	*(.4)*
School Libraries						
Adult Trade Hardbound	46.3	5.10	51.6	*11.4*	5.08	*(.4)*
Adult Trade Paperbound	4.2	1.90	4.8	*14.3*	1.85	*(2.6)*
Juvenile	43.1	12.31	46.1	*7.0*	12.46	*12.2*
Professional	9.2	.61	10.4	*13.0*	.59	*(3.3)*
Mass Market Paperback	18.3	18.30	20.3	*10.9*	18.45	*.8*
Subscription Reference	12.1	.05	13.5	*11.2*	.05	*.4*
Other	7.4	.81	8.2	*10.8*	.81	*0.0*
Total School Libraries	140.6	39.08	154.9	*10.2*	38.29	*.5*
All Libraries	389.9	70.34	430.6	*10.4*	70.69	*.5*

	1974-75			1975-76		
	Dollars	Units		Dollars	Units	
College and University Libraries						
Trade	39.5	.2	2.69 (9.4)	39.9	1.0	2.53 (5.9)
Technical and Scientific	11.3	4.6	.50 (9.1)	11.9	5.3	.48 (4.0)
Business and Other Professional	11.8	4.4	.68 (6.8)	12.4	5.1	.66 (2.9)
Medical	6.2	6.9	.30 (6.3)	6.6	6.5	.29 (3.3)
University Press	12.9	4.0	1.02 (2.9)	13.5	4.7	1.01 (1.0)
Subscription Reference	5.0	2.0	.01 (9.6)	5.3	6.0	.01 .3
Other	4.7	2.2	.42 (6.7)	4.8	2.1	.40 (4.8)
Total College and Univ. Libraries	91.4	3.2	5.62 (8.2)	94.4	3.3	5.38 (4.3)
Public Libraries						
Adult Trade Hardbound	71.2	7.0	6.44 (1.7)	75.3	5.8	6.41 (.5)
Adult Trade Paperbound	3.5	9.4	1.17 (4.9)	3.8	8.6	1.17 0.0
Juvenile	32.9	6.1	8.55 2.2	34.5	4.9	8.63 1.0
Professional	23.1	10.0	1.15 (4.5)	24.7	6.9	1.13 (1.7)
Mass Market Paperback	5.3	8.2	4.53 1.8	5.8	9.4	4.64 2.4
Subscription Reference	8.7	8.7	.03 (2.4)	9.2	5.7	.03 (.1)
Other	9.7	6.6	.87 (3.3)	10.3	6.1	.87 0.0
Total Public Libraries	154.4	7.4	22.74 0.0	163.6	6.0	22.88 .6
Special Libraries						
Trade	3.4	6.2	.28 (3.4)	3.6	5.8	.28 0.0
Religious	2.4	9.1	.31 (3.3)	2.5	4.2	.31 0.0
Technical and Scientific	15.4	10.0	.68 (4.2)	16.5	7.1	.66 (2.9)
Business and Other Professional	10.6	9.2	.61 (1.6)	11.3	6.6	.60 (1.6)
Medical	11.7	9.3	.56 (6.6)	12.5	6.8	.55 (1.8)
Other	3.8	5.5	.06 (5.1)	4.0	5.2	.06 0.0
Total Special Libraries	47.3	9.0	2.50 (3.5)	50.4	6.6	2.46 (1.6)
School Libraries						
Adult Trade Hardbound	51.1 (1.0)		4.62 (9.1)	49.5	(3.1)	4.21 (8.9)
Adult Trade Paperbound	4.6 (4.2)		1.53 (17.3)	4.5	(2.2)	1.38 (9.8)
Juvenile	46.2	.2	12.00 (3.7)	45.7	(1.1)	11.43 (4.8)
Professional	10.3 (1.0)		.51 (13.6)	9.9	(3.9)	.45 (11.8)
Mass Market Paperback	19.9 (2.0)		17.00 (7.9)	19.7	(1.0)	15.76 (7.3)
Subscription Reference	13.4 (.7)		.05 (9.8)	13.0	(3.0)	.04 (8.0)
Other	8.0 (2.4)		.72 (11.1)	7.7	(3.8)	.65 (9.7)
Total School Libraries	153.5 (.9)		36.43 (7.3)	150.0	(2.3)	33.92 (6.9)
All Libraries	446.6	3.7	67.29 (4.8)	458.4	2.6	64.64 (3.9)

	1966-77				1977-78			
	Dollars		Units		Dollars		Units	
College and University Libraries								
Trade	41.9	5.0	2.53	0.0	43.9	4.8	2.53	0.0
Technical and Scientific	12.7	6.7	.48	0.0	13.6	7.1	.48	.9
Business and Other Professional	13.2	6.5	.66	0.0	14.1	6.8	.66	0.0
Medical	7.1	9.2	.29	0.0	7.6	7.0	.29	0.0
University Press	14.4	6.7	1.01	0.0	15.3	6.3	1.02	1.0
Subscription Reference	5.6	5.7	.01	0.0	6.0	7.1	.01	2.0
Other	5.1	6.2	.40	0.0	5.4	5.9	.40	.7
Total College and Univ. Libraries	100.0	5.9	5.38	0.0	105.9	5.9	5.39	.2
Public Libraries								
Adult Trade Hardbound	81.3	-8.0	6.58	2.7	89.5	10.0	6.91	5.0
Adult Trade Paperbound	4.1	7.8	1.19	1.7	4.5	9.8	1.23	3.4
Juvenile	37.9	9.9	9.02	4.2	40.9	7.9	9.30	3.1
Professional	26.7	8.0	1.14	1.0	29.4	10.1	1.18	3.5
Mass Market Paperback	6.4	10.3	4.85	4.5	7.2	12.5	5.14	6.0
Subscription Reference	9.9	7.6	.03	1.9	10.7	8.1	.03	2.7
Other	11.1	7.8	.88	1.1	11.9	7.2	.90	2.2
Total Public Libraries	177.4	8.4	23.69	3.5	194.1	9.4	24.69	4.2
Special Libraries								
Trade	3.8	5.6	.28	0.0	4.1	7.9	.29	3.6
Religious	2.6	4.0	.31	0.0	2.8	7.7	.32	3.2
Technical and Scientific	18.2	10.3	.68	3.0	20.0	10.0	.71	4.4
Business and Other Professional	12.4	9.7	.61	1.7	13.5	8.9	.63	3.3
Medical	13.7	9.6	.56	1.8	14.9	8.8	.57	1.8
Other	4.2	5.0	.06	(1.0)	4.5	7.1	.06	1.3
Total Special Libraries	54.9	8.9	2.50	1.6	59.8	8.9	2.58	3.2
School Libraries								
Adult Trade Hardbound	51.0	3.0	4.13	(1.9)	52.8	3.5	4.08	(1.2)
Adult Trade Paperbound	4.7	4.4	1.36	(1.4)	5.0	6.4	1.37	.7
Juvenile	47.2	3.3	11.24	(1.7)	49.3	4.4	11.20	(.4)
Professional	10.1	2.0	.43	(4.4)	10.6	5.0	.42	(1.5)
Mass Market Paperback	20.5	4.1	15.33	(1.5)	21.7	6.0	15.50	(.2)
Subscription Reference	13.3	2.3	.04	(2.7)	13.7	3.0	.04	(1.8)
Other	7.9	2.6	.63	(3.1)	8.2	3.8	.62	(1.6)
Total School Libraries	154.7	3.1	33.36	(1.7)	161.3	4.3	33.23	(1.0)
All Libraries	487.0	6.2	64.93	.4	521.1	7.0	65.89	1.5

1978-79

	Dollars		Units		% change 1972-73 Dollars	Units
College and University Libraries						
Trade	46.3	5.5	2.55	.7	27.5	(15.6)
Technical and Scientific	14.6	7.4	.49	2.0	49.0	(15.5)
Business and Other Professional	15.1	7.1	.66	.3	46.6	(9.6)
Medical	5.2	7.9	.29	1.1	54.7	(17.1)
University Press	16.3	6.5	1.03	1.0	32.5	(2.8)
Subscription Reference	6.4	6.6	.01	1.7	56.1	(.7)
Other	5.8	7.4	.41	2.5	34.9	(4.7)
Total College and Univ. Libraries	112.7	6.4	5.44	.9	36.8	(12.4)
Public Libraries						
Adult Trade Hardbound	99.3	10.9	7.33	6.1	70.0	14.8
Adult Trade Paperbound	5.0	11.1	1.30	5.7	78.6	2.4
Juvenile	44.6	9.0	9.70	4.3	52.7	16.3
Professional	32.3	9.9	1.21	2.5	76.5	(.8)
Mass Market Paperback	7.9	9.7	5.34	3.9	83.7	24.1
Subscription Reference	11.6	8.4	.03	3.3	61.1	5.4
Other	12.8	7.6	.93	3.3	54.2	2.1
Total Public Libraries	213.5	10.0	25.84	4.7	66.1	15.1
Special Libraries						
Trade	4.4	7.3	.30	3.4	41.4	0.0
Religious	3.0	7.1	.32	2.5	40.0	10.3
Technical and Scientific	22.1	10.5	.74	4.2	65.2	(1.4)
Business and Other Professional	14.9	10.4	.65	3.2	55.7	1.6
Medical	16.4	10.1	.59	3.5	62.0	(6.6)
Other	4.9	8.9	.06	3.4	36.4	(1.4)
Total Special Libraries	65.7	9.9	2.66	3.1	55.7	(.8)
School Libraries						
Adult Trade Hardbound	56.2	6.4	4.12	1.0	21.4	(19.2)
Adult Trade Paperbound	5.4	8.0	1.40	.6	28.6	26.3
Juvenile	52.8	7.1	11.48	2.5	22.5	(6.7)
Professional	11.3	6.6	.42	0.0	22.8	(31.1)
Mass Market Paperback	23.6	8.8	15.95	2.9	29.0	(12.8)
Subscription Reference	14.6	6.6	.04	1.8	20.7	(19.0)
Other	8.8	7.3	.64	3.2	18.9	(20.0)
Total School Libraries	172.7	7.1	34.05	2.5	22.8	(12.9)
All Libraries	564.6	8.3	67.99	3.2	33.6	(6.3)

Appendix.VIII:

Estimated Acquisitions by U.S. Schools of General Books and Audiovisual Materials 1972-73 to 1978-79
(MILLIONS OF DOLLARS AND UNITS)

Figures in italics represent percentage changes from previous year; parentheses show decline

| | 1972-73 | | 1973-74 | | | |
	Dollars	Units	Dollars		Units	
Books (Total)	192.2	72.99	212.6	*10.6*	73.89	*1.2*
Adult Trade Hardbound	50.4	5.51	55.9	*10.9*	5.51	*0.0*
Adult Trade Paperbound	12.0	5.45	13.9	*15.8*	5.35	*(1.8)*
Juvenile	49.3	14.09	52.5	*6.5*	14.19	*.7*
Professional	10.1	.67	11.6	*14.9*	.66	*.66*
Mass Market Paperback	46.0	46.00	51.6	*12.2*	46.91	*2.0*
Subscription Reference	13.3	.06	14.8	*11.2*	.06	*0.0*
Other	11.1	1.21	12.3	*10.8*	1.21	*0.0*
Audiovisuals	187.2	11.34	221.1	*18.1*	11.17	*(1.5)*
Total Books & AV	379.4	84.33	433.7	*14.3*	85.06	*.9*

| | 1974-75 | | | 1975-76 | | |
	Dollars		Units	Dollars		Units
Books (Total)	210.7	*(.9)*	69.40 *(6.1)*	205.6	*(2.4)*	63.96 *(7.8)*
Adult Trade Hardbound	54.2	*(3.0)*	4.90 *(11.1)*	52.6	*(3.0)*	4.48 *(8.5)*
Adult Trade Paperbound	13.7	*(1.4)*	4.57 *(14.6)*	13.4	*(2.2)*	4.12 *(9.8)*
Juvenile	52.8	*.6*	13.71 *(3.4)*	51.8	*(1.9)*	12.95 *(5.5)*
Professional	11.4	*(1.7)*	.57 *(13.6)*	11.1	*(2.6)*	.51 *(10.5)*
Mass Market Paperback	52.1	*.9*	44.53 *(5.1)*	51.1	*(1.9)*	40.88 *(8.2)*
Subscription Reference	14.6	*(1.3)*	.05 *(10.3)*	14.1	*(3.4)*	.05 *(8.4)*
Other	11.9	*(3.2)*	1.07 *(11.6)*	11.5	*(3.4)*	.97 *(9.3)*
Audiovisuals	213.5	*(3.4)*	9.14 *(18.2)*	211.4	*(1.0)*	8.31 *(9.1)*
Total Books & AV	424.2	*(2.2)*	78.54 *(7.7)*	417.0	*(1.7)*	72.27 *(8.0)*

	1976-77				1977-78			
	Dollars		Units		Dollars		Units	
Books (Total)	209.4	1.8	61.82	(3.3)	215.9	3.1	60.32	(2.4)
Adult Trade Hardbound	53.5	1.7	4.33	(3.3)	55.1	3.0	4.25	(1.8)
Adult Trade Paperbound	13.7	2.2	3.97	(3.6)	14.2	3.6	3.89	(2.0)
Juvenile	52.9	2.1	12.60	(2.7)	54.5	3.0	12.39	(1.7)
Professional	11.2	.9	.47	(7.8)	11.6	3.6	.46	(2.1)
Mass Market Paperback	52.1	1.9	39.47	(3.4)	53.7	3.1	38.36	(2.8)
Subscription Reference	14.3	1.4	.05	(3.6)	14.7	2.8	.05	(2.0)
Other	11.7	1.7	.93	(4.1)	12.1	3.4	.92	(1.1)
Audiovisuals	216.7	2.5	8.26	(.6)	224.9	3.8	7.89	(4.5)
Total Books & AV	426.1	2.2	70.08	(3.0)	440.8	4.2	68.21	(2.7)

	1978-79				% change 1972-73	
	Dollars		Units		Dollars	Units
Books (Total)	228.3	5.7	60.62	.5	18.8	(16.9)
Adult Trade Hardbound	58.1	5.4	4.29	.9	15.3	(22.1)
Adult Trade Paperbound	15.0	5.6	3.90	.3	25.0	(28.4)
Juvenile	57.7	5.9	12.54	1.2	17.0	(11.0)
Professional	12.3	6.0	.46	0.0	21.8	(31.3)
Mass Market Paperback	56.9	6.0	38.45	.2	23.7	(16.4)
Subscription Reference	15.5	5.4	.05	.7	16.5	(21.7)
Other	12.8	5.8	.93	1.1	15.3	(23.1)
Audiovisuals	239.5	6.5	7.98	1.1	27.9	(29.6)
Total Books & AV	467.8	6.1	68.60	.6	23.3	(18.7)

Created by John P. Dessauer, Reprinted from the June 16, 1975 issue of *Publishers Weekly*, published by R. R. Bowker Company, a Xerox company, Copyright © 1975 by Xerox Corporation.

Appendix IX:

**Estimated Average Unit Costs Incurred by U.S. Schools
for General Books and Audiovisual Materials
1972-73 to 1978-79 (DOLLARS)**

Figures in italics represent percentage increases from previous year

	1972-73	1973-74	
	Dollars	Dollars	
Books (Total)	2.63	2.88	*9.5*
Adult Trade Hardbound	9.15	10.15	*10.9*
Adult Trade Paperbound	2.20	2.60	*18.1*
Juvenile	3.50	3.70	*5.7*
Professional	15.00	17.50	*16.6*
Mass Market Paperback	1.00	1.10	*10.0*
Subscription Reference	225.00	250.00	*11.1*
Other	9.15	10.15	*10.9*
Audiovisuals	16.50	19.80	*20.0*
Total Books & AV	4.50	5.10	*13.3*

	1974-75		1975-76	
	Dollars		Dollars	
Books (Total)	3.04	*5.6*	3.21	*5.6*
Adult Trade Hardbound	11.05	*8.9*	11.75	*6.3*
Adult Trade Paperbound	3.00	*15.4*	3.25	*8.3*
Juvenile	3.85	*4.0*	4.00	*3.9*
Professional	20.15	*15.1*	21.95	*8.9*
Mass Market Paperback	1.17	*6.4*	1.25	*6.8*
Subscription Reference	275.00	*10.0*	290.00	*5.5*
Other	11.15	*9.9*	11.85	*6.3*
Audiovisuals	23.35	*17.9*	25.45	*9.0*
Total Books & AV	5.40	*5.9*	5.77	*6.9*

	1976-77		1977-78	
	Dollars		Dollars	
Books (Total)	3.39	5.6	3.58	5.6
Adult Trade Hardbound	12.35	5.1	12.95	4.9
Adult Trade Paperbound	3.45	6.2	3.65	5.8
Juvenile	4.20	5.0	4.40	4.8
Professional	23.45	6.8	25.00	6.6
Mass Market Paperback	1.32	5.6	1.40	6.0
Subscription Reference	305.00	5.2	320.00	4.9
Other	12.55	5.9	13.15	4.8
Audiovisuals	27.00	6.0	28.50	5.5
Total Books & AV	6.08	5.4	6.41	6.3

	1978-79		% change 1972-73
	Dollars		Dollars
Books (Total)	377	5.3	43.3
Adult Trade Hardbound	13.55	4.6	48.1
Adult Trade Paperbound	3.85	5.5	75.0
Juvenile	4.60	4.5	31.4
Professional	26.65	6.6	77.7
Market Paperback	1.48	5.7	48.0
Subscription Reference	335.00	4.7	48.9
Other	13.80	4.9	50.8
Audiovisuals	30.00	5.3	81.8
Total Books & AV	6.82	5.6	51.6

Appendix X:

Estimated Comparative Materials Expenditures by U.S. Libraries 1972-73 and 1978-79
(MILLIONS OF DOLLARS)

	EXPENDITURES			% share of all divisional expenditures		% share of all library expenditures	
	Dollars		% change				
	1972-73	1978-79	79 from 73	1972-73	1978-79	1972-73	1978-79
Books—Domestic							
College and University Libraries	82.4	112.7	36.8	25.5	23.0	8.4	7.6
Public Libraries	128.5	213.5	66.1	70.6	68.8	13.1	14.5
Special Libraries	38.4	65.7	71.1	24.1	23.0	3.9	4.4
School Libraries	140.6	172.7	22.8	44.7	44.0	14.4	11.7
All Libraries	389.9	564.6	44.8	39.8	38.2	39.8	38.2
Books—Imports							
College and University Libraries	56.9	86.6	52.2	17.6	17.6	5.8	5.8
Public Libraries	3.1	5.8	87.1	1.7	1.9	.3	.4
Special Libraries	22.7	40.8	79.7	14.2	14.3	2.4	2.8
All Libraries	82.7	133.2	61.1	8.5	9.0	8.5	9.0
Books—Government & Special							
College and University Libraries	15.3	22.6	47.7	4.8	4.6	1.6	1.5
Public Libraries	5.3	9.0	69.8	2.9	2.9	.5	.6
Special Libraries	7.0	11.9	70.0	4.4	4.2	.7	.8
All Libraries	27.6	43.5	57.6	2.8	2.9	2.8	2.9
Books—Total							
College and University Libraries	154.6	221.9	43.5	47.9	45.2	15.8	15.0
Public Libraries	136.9	228.3	66.8	75.2	73.6	14.0	15.4
Special Libraries	68.1	118.4	73.9	42.7	41.5	6.9	8.0
School Libraries	140.6	172.7	22.8	44.7	44.0	14.4	11.7
All Libraries	500.2	741.3	48.2	51.1	50.1	51.1	50.1
Periodicals							
College and University Libraries	106.6	174.4	63.6	33.0	35.5	10.9	11.8
Public Libraries	16.2	30.3	87.0	8.9	9.8	1.6	2.1
Special Libraries	58.8	112.0	90.5	36.9	39.3	6.0	7.6
School Libraries	18.4	22.8	23.9	5.8	5.8	1.9	1.5
All Libraries	200.0	339.5	69.8	20.4	23.0	20.4	23.0
Audiovisuals							
College and University Libraries	19.4	28.8	48.5	6.0	5.9	2.0	2.0
Public Libraries	16.7	31.0	85.6	9.2	10.0	1.7	2.1
Special Libraries	9.5	16.9	77.9	6.0	5.9	1.0	1.1
School Libraries	149.7	190.2	27.1	47.6	48.5	15.3	12.9
All Libraries	195.3	266.9	36.7	20.0	18.1	20.0	18.1
Microform							
College and University Libraries	19.3	30.5	58.0	6.0	6.2	2.0	2.0
Public Libraries	6.0	10.5	75.0	3.3	3.4	.6	.7
Special Libraries	11.7	20.3	73.5	7.3	7.1	1.2	1.4
School Libraries	4.9	5.8	18.4	1.6	1.5	.5	.4
All Libraries	41.9	67.1	60.1	4.3	4.5	4.3	4.5
Binding							
College and University Libraries	22.8	35.1	53.9	7.1	7.2	2.3	2.4
Public Libraries	6.1	10.0	63.9	3.4	3.2	.6	.7
Special Libraries	11.3	17.5	54.9	7.1	6.2	1.2	1.2
School Libraries	1.0	1.0	11.1	.3	.2	.1	.0
All Libraries	41.2	63.6	54.4	4.2	4.3	4.2	4.3
Total Expenditures							
College and University Libraries	322.7	490.7	52.1	100.0	100.0	33.0	33.2
Public Libraries	181.9	310.1	70.5	100.0	100.0	18.6	21.0
Special Libraries	159.4	285.1	78.9	100.0	100.0	16.3	19.3
School Libraries	314.6	392.5	24.8	100.0	100.0	32.1	26.5
All Libraries	978.6	1,478.4	51.1	100.0	100.0	100.0	100.0

Index